MY LIFE
in pictures

ANDREW

FLINTOFF
MY LIFE
in pictures

ANDREW FLINTOFF
WITH **PATRICK MURPHY**

PHOTOGRAPHS BY
GRAHAM MORRIS

ORION

Contents

Introduction

Andrew Flintoff doing a book at the tender age of 26? A tad premature, surely? Given his statistical record since first playing Test cricket at 20, that's fair comment. Yet there's something about Flintoff that defies trenchant critical examination. In these days of cloned England cricketers, where most of their public comments and actions on the field are from the same narrow prism, Flintoff stands out as a genuine individual – and not just in the way that he plays cricket.

One of the rare times I've submitted myself to a fashion shoot. London's West End, early in 2004 – decent threads though!

Just ask picture desk editors on the national newspapers or all the lifestyle magazines if they think Andrew Flintoff is worth the candle. They believe he's charismatic, entertaining and reaches the parts that other, worthier but duller, cricketers can't reach. Flintoff tickles the advertising industry's 'G' spot and those reactionaries who bemoan the attention given to him, despite a modest international record so far, ought to wise up. Those sceptics probably thought that Ian Botham didn't deserve all the attention, that he got his early stack of wickets and runs against weak opposition and that he was just a slogger who bluffed his way to stardom.

Yes, Ian Botham. Let's get the analogy with England's greatest all-rounder out of the way early. You'd need a prolonged lie-down in a darkened room to suggest that Flintoff has achieved the same sort of stature yet. At the same age – 26 – Botham had taken more than 200 Test wickets and scored ten centuries, while for Flintoff the tally is just over 60 and three.

Yet Flintoff's impact on cricket crowds is now as galvanic as at any time since Botham was in his heyday more than 20 years ago. Flintoff empties bars when he comes in to bat. He's four inches taller than Botham and, now that he's at last grasped the need for prolonged and consistent fitness work, more athletic and tapered in his body than the great roisterer. Flintoff's bat appears the size of a toothpick in his massive mitts. He clearly feels he now belongs on the highest stage after years of setbacks and pitfalls – some of them his own doing. In comparison, Botham's rise and rise from 1977 onwards was a gilded passage. It also helped that he stayed fit enough to get on the park.

No one in world cricket hits the ball harder than Flintoff. England bowlers in the nets make their excuses, hoping they can work in the adjoining net in order to avoid fractures as the ball rockets back at them. His fielding in the deep is superior to Botham's, with a stronger arm and deceptive speed across the ground. At second slip, they are on a par, prehensile and inspirational.

Flintoff's controlled, brutal batting against the South Africans in the 2003 Test series marked out his progress to maturity. It wasn't just the calculated judgement involved, averaging 52, nor the effect he had on the crowds – especially at Lord's and The Oval – but the wary acceptance from the opposition

The days are gone when I have to worry about being caught climbing into a curry in public.
No pints of lager with this one – Durban in 1999 at Christmas. I've probably come straight from the hotel gym!

that Flintoff was now a special cricketer, a match-winner. Like Botham, Flintoff was now shaping matches, bending them to his will.

You can dismiss these observations as the deluded ramblings of someone who has broadcast on England's failings all around the world and who just desires to be entertained in his broadcasting dotage. But pay closer attention to the views of his former Lancashire and England colleague, Mike Atherton, a man not easily lured into hyperbole. 'He can win games single-handedly and that's something England desperately need. Like Botham, he draws people into cricket. He has the same bear hug for his team-mates when someone does well on the field. He is a caring, giving man to the team ethic. And the effect he has on the crowd when he walks in is Bothamesque. He'll disappoint his admirers a few times in the future, because that's the way he plays, but he'll always be fun to watch.'

'Fun to watch.' A phrase that too often slips out of the international sportsman's lexicon. Not Flintoff. He knows that he has got himself out gormlessly in big games and will do so again – but now he has the mental strength to keep playing the way that suits him. It certainly suits his current England captain, Michael Vaughan: 'It's best just to tell him not to worry if he fails now and again, to stick to his game plan. All he needs to do is to keep focusing in the way he has done in the past year and keep practising, because he has an amazing ability and you should never doubt that.'

Andrew Flintoff always had tremendous natural ability. From the age of eight, he was playing way beyond his age group, graduating from every England under-age side to the Test team at the age of 20. He gave tantalising glimpses of his massive talent in his rollercoaster journey towards maturity as an international cricketer. One came in July 2000 when he played a remarkable innings of 135 not out against Surrey, the best bowling side in the country, at The Oval. It was the quarter-final of the NatWest Trophy and Flintoff simply dismissed the bowlers from his presence. They included the brilliant Pakistani spinner Saqlain Mushtaq, at the time, good enough for any batsman in the world, with his accuracy and subtle variations. Not that day. Flintoff got his runs off 111 balls, with exactly a hundred of them coming in boundaries – not one of them a false or a frenetic stroke.

David Gower, who was commentating for television on that Oval match, said: 'We have just watched one of the most awesome innings we are ever going to

MUTTIAH MURALITHARAN

Lancashire team-mate of Flintoff and Sri Lankan spin bowler

'He can be one of the great all-rounders for the next ten years. He's the danger man for the opposition because he can turn the game around in an hour. When we talk about facing England, he's the one we fear.'

see on a cricket field.' That's David Gower, the master of understatement when it comes to assessing a player's worth. Mike Atherton, a man in similar mould, played for Lancashire that day and recalls the relevance of that Flintoff innings. 'He won it against the best side in the country off his own bat. He dominated Saqlain, which was very rare in those days. Having a decisive impact on a match that matters is the hallmark of an important cricketer and that was a strong pointer to his potential.' Flintoff was just 22 at the time.

So it's understandable that after an innings like that, the burden of expectation would sit heavily on the precocious Flintoff. Through all the vicissitudes of form and fitness, he has been harder on himself than anyone else. Now, after a year of hard technical work with the Lancashire coach Mike Watkinson and a more responsible attitude to keeping supremely fit, his batting is falling into place at last. 'I don't try to hammer the ball so hard now; I look to time it, caress it. The shot that goes straight past the bowler at a rate of knots is a demoralising one for the bowler, as I know from experience – and that one's going well for me. But I still like hitting the ball out of the ground! It's a case of biding my time, not getting tempted too soon. I'm lucky that I'm strong enough to miss-hit the ball to the boundary, but I get angry at myself then. I'm looking just to ping it.'

One final cricketing comparison with Ian Botham: Flintoff's fast bowling is clearly inferior to Botham's devastating ability to swing the ball at pace when he was at his peak. He has taken just two five-wicket hauls in first-class cricket. Yet Flintoff is seriously quick when he slips himself – in the common coaching parlance 'he bowls a heavy ball' – and he is rarely collared. His willingness to bowl long spells, uphill or into the wind, makes him invaluable for his captain and he is particularly effective against left-handers, as he angles the ball into them. He lacks Botham's supreme ability to move the ball away late from the right-hander and the great man's knack of conjuring wickets from nowhere. Flintoff is an unlucky bowler, suffering from dropped catches and operating at unfavourable times in an innings, but he is valued by his captains.

Michael Vaughan rates him highly. 'I believe that sooner or later he's going to get a big, big haul of wickets in a period of play and not just in one game, but

DAVID LLOYD
Flintoff's coach at Lancashire, then England

'He's such a popular cricketer, because he's a great entertainer but not selfish. His commitment to the team is fantastic; he loves to see another one of the lads do well. He loves a prank and a laugh but gets the marriage right between enjoying himself and not upsetting anyone. A coach wants to know if a player can win a game, taking it away from the opposition. This lad can.'

in a series or year. I think he's that good a bowler, but we do have to be careful how we bowl him.' Flintoff's adherence to the team ethic and his uncomplaining nature may count against him when the overs clock up. They have done so already with England. But Vaughan's awareness of that bodes well for Flintoff's continuance in the pivotal role of all-rounder. There have been too many false dawns in his international career for either player or management to risk too many spells when it's not necessary.

He is now the heartbeat of the England side, like Darren Gough a few years ago before injury ravaged his right knee. He shares Gough's ability to

There's always room for a bit of a laugh before training.

laugh at himself, and to gee up the more introspective members of the team. Both have enjoyed the social aspect of the game and their popularity has extended beyond the narrow boundaries inhabited by cricket lovers. They are natural communicators, radiating their pleasure at playing the game for a living, aware of the crowd's involvement. Many contemporary England cricketers talk about 'being in the bubble', impervious to anything else that's happening away from their own professional world, especially on tour. Not Gough and, mercifully, not Flintoff.

In March 2002, one of our media corps was set to get married after England's tour of New Zealand. Flintoff was the only England player to be invited to the stag night in Wellington. As it was staged two days before the third Test, Flintoff limited himself to just one glass of wine all night, but he had an important function to perform. In common with most stag nights, the guests were made to drink vast quantities of booze in forfeits. Whenever one of our party transgressed, to great hilarity, Flintoff would stretch out a massive left paw, drag back a quivering neck and pour down a generous shot of tequila. No one would argue with Flintoff, but he carried out his punitive duties with great humour. Despite his abstemious evening, he was the life and soul of the party and cemented his popularity with some of those present who barely knew him.

A few days later, I had personal experience of his thoughtful nature. In common with everyone on that tour, we were all shocked and saddened at the death of Ben Hollioake in a car crash. Flintoff had known Hollioake for years; they had played for under-age England teams, then the seniors together. He was understandably shattered. At the end of the Test, after he had bludgeoned one of the fastest fifties ever in Tests by an Englishman, he declined to do an interview with

Believe it or not, I do think about how I've batted after a session in the nets. I've always taken practice seriously.

My natural agility will insist on coming out – even in an England training session! What back problem?

NEIL FAIRBROTHER

former Lancashire team-mate and now his business manager

'When he bats he's now like the Australians in the way that they are so aggressive. He instantly puts the bowlers on the back foot. These days you must dominate as a batter in Test cricket and his range of shots is so wide, and he is so destructive that he could just play within himself and score 150 in the day.'

me for BBC Radio. When I returned to my hotel room an hour later, he'd left me a message saying that he was so upset at Hollioake's death that he would have struggled to sound coherent. He hoped I'd understand and that he'd buy me a beer next day as apology. That remains the only time an England player has taken the trouble to explain why one of my requests was knocked back.

There is much more to Andrew Flintoff than a brawny Lancastrian with a ready grin and fetching diamond earring. At an age when many lads are boogieing away to cacophonous rubbish like garage, rap or hip-hop, he plays Radio Two. He admires Terry Wogan and Ken Bruce, listens unashamedly to Steve Wright's *Sunday Love Songs* and is word-perfect on legendary artists from the sixties such as Dusty Springfield, the Beatles and Dean Martin. He's a huge fan of Frank Sinatra, devouring books on that complex man, and Elvis Presley is his singing idol. 'He died the year I was born – 1977 – and I love his music. On my wall at home I've got a signed album cover of *Loving You*, with a certificate of authentication. I just think that Sinatra, Martin and that whole Rat Pack thing was so cool, and they could sing. I prefer melody to all that stuff the England lads play. It's like someone's stuck

Showing off my car, a black Jaguar S-type, three litre sports. It's comfortable, stylish and has enough pace. Plus a CD–player and that woman who gives you instructions when you haven't got a clue where you're going. A bit of a contrast to my first car when I joined the staff at Lancashire – a Fiat Uno.

MICHAEL VAUGHAN

England captain

'He's always at the centre of things and that's going to happen even more now. He's a big player. He stands at second slip and if you have someone there who's keeping the team going that's a massive help for the captain. The word's got around that Flintoff's matured and has become the cricketer that he's been promising to become for a few years. They are aware that Flintoff can win England a game and they realise that when he comes to the crease that it's quite a crucial period for them.'

With my boxer dog, Fred. I've got another one called Arnold. Why boxers? I got a book when I decided I wanted a dog and it said that boxers are alert and sharp, with a lifelong puppyish behaviour. Bit like myself, I thought.

your head down a dustbin, and then banged the lid down on you. Radio Two gives you a wide array of music, and I like Wogan's bright, sarcastic humour.'

He has played chess from the age of ten, representing Lancashire Schools. The cerebral Mike Atherton was unaware of this when the teenage Flintoff joined the Lancashire seniors on a preseason tour to Jamaica. Atherton asked Flintoff if he played, was surprised to be given the nod and even more wrong-footed when the youngster beat the Cambridge graduate. Atherton hasn't asked Flintoff for a game since!

Although he relishes the vocal support of the crowd, feeding off them to boost adrenalin even further, he is shy in the company of people he doesn't really know. When he appeared on BBC TV's *Question of Sport* – confirmation that you've really arrived in sport – he felt ill at ease and nervous, aware that he had little in common with the others. Flintoff doesn't relish the celebrity syndrome, resisting the opportunity to cash in on his enhanced, instantly recognisable status. He is bright, sharp-witted but grounded, happy in his Lancashire roots, determined to remain consistent with friends he knows and trusts. Judgement in social matters was not his forte when younger, as he admits, but with a loving, developing relationship with his fiancée Rachael has come an awareness that a quiet night in with the CD collection has its attractions.

This is now the best period of Andrew Flintoff's life. It remains to be seen how far he will kick on as a cricketer. Those who doubt his credentials to prosper at the highest level will point at a modest statistical return so far. So far. After the same number of Tests as Flintoff, Mark Butcher was averaging 28, yet he then progressed through the gears so that he is now an integral part of England's Test side. It took Steve Waugh 26 Tests before he scored his first hundred, at the same age as Flintoff. It would be foolish to suggest that Flintoff could achieve the legendary stature of Waugh before he shuffles off, but there's no doubt his figures at present don't reflect his talents as an all-rounder.

And he hasn't breezed through his early England years in the manner of a Gower or a Botham. There have been many rebuffs and pratfalls along the way. He was in pain through a chronic back problem for eight years, throughout his teens. In some seasons he didn't deliver a ball. He made two noughts in the same match in just his second Test, at the age of 20. He was pilloried for being heavier than the boxer Lennox Lewis in his *annus horribilis* of 2000, when someone in the England management hung him out to dry, leaking their dissatisfaction to the media without taking the player to one side. In the 2001 Test series in India, he couldn't get a run, shedding tears of frustration in the dressing room at getting out limply in the final Test. His willingness to bowl so many overs in the 2002 home series against India cost him a double hernia, a serious operation and months of unrelentingly hard work, after he'd been forced to come home early from the Ashes tour, in a desperate bid to get fit for the World Cup.

Not even those who judge Andrew Flintoff most rigorously can begrudge him his time in the sun now. There is no more genial England cricketer around, none more flamboyant, no bigger team man and none more popular with the paying customers, and with those who know little about cricket, but relish a personality who transcends a mere cricket match.

PATRICK MURPHY
May 2004

MARK BUTCHER
England team-mate

'Test cricket's a very difficult game and some don't take to it as quickly as they'd like. We are both in that category. But that South African series at home [in 2003] showed what all his team-mates believe he will do on a regular basis from now on. He's also a complete idol to the crowds.'

Obliging the autograph hunters in Sri Lanka, with Michael Vaughan in the background.

CHAPTER 1

A Lancashire Lad

These days Andrew Flintoff enjoys most of the social accoutrements of the successful international sportsman. He is settled snugly in a comfortable home down a quiet country lane in Cheshire with his fiancée Rachael. Their first baby is on the way and an elegant Jaguar car is parked on the gravel path. He employs a respectable agent, possesses a central contract with England and a sizeable wardrobe containing some fashionable threads that wouldn't have fitted the generous Flintoff torso of a year or two back. He is now at the happiest stage of his life, personally and professionally. He may have dined at the Ivy in London's West End, chatting to Michael Caine as he passed by the actor's table; he may have taken the air on a yacht or two while on England tours – but he is still Freddie Flintoff from Preston. Above all, he knows just how close he came to losing out on maximising the massive potential that was so obvious to many good judges of the game from as far back as the age of nine.

Back at my first cricket club in Preston – Dutton Forshaw, where my dad and brother also played.

At his best, Flintoff makes batting and fielding look particularly easy. The fast bowling, although developing in range and shrewdness, requires more effort and brawn. But Flintoff is aware that he owes much to those who kept faith with him through all the injuries, poor form and under-achievement. That's why he's determined to stay grounded.

'Loyalty is important to me. I'll never forget where I've come from and who I owe a lot to for helping me get to this stage of my career and my life. My memories of growing up in Preston are very fond and warm. My parents made great sacrifices for me, and so did many who invested time and encouragement in me. Like so many in the world of cricket who never get a mention, they just get on with the job quietly and don't look for thanks.'

He has been called Freddie since joining Lancashire County Cricket Club at the age of 15. Cricketers aren't known for many imaginative nicknames – isn't that right Vaughany/Trezz/Butch? – and Flintoff's owed everything to the TV cartoon character Fred Flintstone. But Freddie Flintoff has a warm, accessible air to it and a spot of alliteration never hurt anyone.

Freddie fits easily back into his Preston skin when he returns there, despite the status he has achieved in his chosen career, playing for a high-profile county, at a famous ground next door to the most famous football club in the world. He relishes the easy banter from mates he has known for years and expects to be treated in the same down-to-earth manner.

'When I go back to see my parents or have a drink with my old mates at the New Friargate Social Club, I'm determined that nobody will ever think I'm giving it the Billy Big-Time. Having a few quiet ones, enjoying a game of pool, remembering how everyone sits in the same spot every night, getting my leg pulled – I love all that. When I meet famous people from other walks of life, I'm usually shy and quiet. I stick to what I know and who I know. When you've experienced the ups and downs I've been through, you take nothing for granted.'

He was quiet and shy at school, which may surprise those who see him as an expansive character, relishing the limelight on the public stage. But it's only cricket that has brought him self-confidence and social assurance.

'I never thought I'd make a living from cricket until I was taken on the staff at Old Trafford. I had no clear ambition to be a professional sportsman at school, even though I was good at games. You didn't think of doing a GCSE in PE around Preston in those days! But I got nine GCSEs, so I wasn't exactly a duffer. My brother Chris was the academic one. He ended up qualifying as a teacher and spent four years working out in Japan.'

Preston has a proud tradition of nurturing top sportsmen. There's Frank Hayes, who scored a Test hundred on his debut and played for many years for Lancashire. Mark Lawrenson, the excellent Liverpool footballer and now resident pundit for the BBC, comes from the town. But the most famous sporting son remains the great Sir Tom Finney – loyal, one-club man, wonderfully versatile forward and an exemplary sportsman. Sir Tom still lives in Preston and is president of the football club he graced with such distinction. He is Flintoff's ideal sportsman.

'I've met him a few times. A lovely, modest man, he's the sort of sportsman you aspire to becoming yourself: someone never too big for his boots.'

That's an ideal that Flintoff often returns to when talking about his contemporaries in cricket or in other sports. He would be hurt if someone he respected thought the glamour of his standing and lifestyle had turned his head.

Although Flintoff played football to an acceptable standard – 'a few games up front for Preston Schools then centre half in the Preston League, and believe it or not I was quite fast!' – he is not a big fan of the sport.

With my brother Chris, who's three years older than me. I'm the one on the right with curls.

'I prefer rugby, where they just get on with it. In football, there's too much hassling of the referees and too much cheating for my liking. I hate to see them rolling around the ground, apparently in agony, then running away without any kind of embarrassment. There doesn't seem to be much loyalty either to a club, as Tom Finney showed to Preston. I couldn't imagine playing for any other county but Lancashire. If ever I got the chance to captain Lancashire full-time I'd be so proud.'

Cricket was the sport that coursed through the Flintoff genes. His brother Chris was a good batsman who still holds the record for his club side in Preston – 213 for Harris Park, playing in the Moore and Smalley Palace Shield League, which operates within a 30-mile radius of Blackpool. Freddie believes Chris would have played at a decent level if he hadn't concentrated on his studies at a key period in his teens and their father, Colin agrees. 'If Chris had put his mind to it, he could've reached at least Minor Counties standard but he was happy to stay and play in the same team as his mates. Then he went off to do economics at Lancaster University, so he wasn't totally into improving himself as a batsman.'

Colin still plays, even though he's in his fifties. He turns out for a village side, Whittingham and Goosenargh. By his own admission he is a nudger and nurdler with the bat and stands at slip, shouting 'Yours!' to his younger teammates. His youngest son, Andrew smiles indulgently at his dad's efforts. 'He plays the percentages, just nudging the ball around. I'm still waiting to find out how you do all that.'

DAVID LLOYD

the Lancashire coach who signed Flintoff

'I think I probably embarrassed Freddie by going on about his qualities to the senior players in those days. But I felt a responsibility, having sat in his parents' front room and sold Lancashire to them. I suppose I treated him like a son. He's always been unbelievably polite and respectful to me whenever we've seen each other in later years and I admit I've got a soft spot for him. I admit that's coloured my judgement at times. The Lancashire lads used to tell me that I'd have him opening the batting and bowling at both ends one day!'

Andrew was just six when he played his first game of cricket and watched his brother and father play on Saturdays, waiting for the chance to get a game with them at Dutton Forshaw Cricket Club. He made it into the junior side at the age of nine and next year followed Chris into the same XI. For one season, Flintoff Senior was joined in the same team by his two sons. 'I was the captain, but that had nothing to do with it. We wanted to introduce youngsters into the club and they were both good enough. Andrew was only 12 when he played with the seniors. I remember him taking 3 for 2 in ten overs for the second XI in that first season.' Colin made only one century in his career, against Gregson Lane's 2nd XI, and Chris was batting with him at the time he got to his hundred, with Andrew also playing that day.

Clearly, Colin Flintoff handled his younger son's cricket development admirably.

'Dad was very good with me. He encouraged me in the right way, letting me enjoy myself, not getting down on me when I failed. He wasn't one of those parents who embarrass you by shouting from the boundary, making you just want to hide away. He must have spotted something in me, because at the age of nine, he organised coaching for me.'

Soon the grapevine of Lancashire CCC had picked up that there was a young lad called Flintoff from Preston who might have something about him. Although skinny, young Freddie was tall and well co-ordinated earlier than his contemporaries. His fielding was already highly impressive, with those bucket hands reliably safe.

Bowling in the second Test in Harare for England Under-19s against Zimbabwe in 1997. There wasn't a lot of meat on me in those days!

Those coaching clinics on Sunday afternoons helped improve his game, giving him greater self-confidence. Soon he was playing for Lancashire Under-11s and a year later went on his first overseas tour – to Argentina with Lancashire Under-16s. Young Flintoff had started on a precocious passage through the various grades, always playing with team-mates who were that much older than him, from Lancashire all the way through the various age groups with England.

'I'd barely played a game of cricket at school, possibly two a summer. It was usually ten Asian lads and me, and there was no real encouragement there. So I was very lucky to have the back-up of my family, club cricket and Lancashire helping me develop. It was just a case of enjoying it; no one banged on about what I should be aiming for. I realise now that a few good judges must have seen my potential, but they did well not to pressurise me.'

The first pressure he encountered came at the age of 12 and it was to have a significant effect on Flintoff's physical development. One of his coaches felt that his bowling action should be altered to enable him to swing it more. Those who have grown used to the sight of Flintoff lumbering to the crease and hurl-

MIKE WATKINSON
Lancashire team-mate and now the coach

'His most difficult period was getting out of schoolboy cricket, then adapting and pushing on when he got onto our staff. Soon people start asking what's he done over the past two seasons. We knew all about his massive potential, but it was a case of adapting to the professional environment. Freddie hasn't had an easy ride along the way. He's had to graft at the coalface.'

ing the ball down with massive effort and limited technical finesse will be surprised to discover that at the age of 12, he had the classical, sideways-on bowling action, straight out of the MCC Coaching Manual. But he was told that he needed to be more chest-on to achieve greater swing-bowling expertise. That alteration coincided with back problems that dogged Flintoff for almost the next decade, through to his early days with the full England side. Now, it may be that the tall, gangly youngster who liked to bowl as fast as possible may have developed a bad back whether or not his action stayed the same. Growing teenagers do get back problems, whether or not they play cricket.

Proof that I didn't always try to hit the cover off the ball when I was a youngster! England Under-19s against Zimbabwe at Southampton in 1997.

But Flintoff's subsequent progress as a fast bowler was undoubtedly checked by his suspect back. It flared up badly at the age of 14 on the day he made his debut for England.

'It was for the Under-15s against Wales and I had to come off the field, because my back was troubling me so much. Ben Hollioake, who was also making his debut that day, was in the same boat, so my abiding memory will always be sitting alongside Ben, waiting for my dad to drive us to see a physiotherapist. Both Ben and I would have to get used to such visits down the years.'

Flintoff didn't bowl for another three years after that match. He grew even taller, but his body didn't fill out in proportion so he was advised to ease the strain on it by just concentrating on his batting. They said he'd be stronger when older and therefore able to resume bowling. He wasn't unduly bothered at the time because batting was so enjoyable, but it was the start of a long, painful association with back pain.

'It lasted for the next eight years, and I got fed up with scans and various diagnoses that were contradictory. The back injury would put extra strain on my groin when I bowled, so that became another worry. None of the scans ever showed up anything serious like a stress fracture and I got very concerned. At one stage I wanted to find a problem so that it could be treated and healed. In time, my back got stronger as I worked harder at my fitness, but it definitely hampered any notions about being an all-rounder through my teens and in my early days as an England player.'

He was so raw as a fast bowler when he joined the Lancashire staff that he didn't even have a proper run-up. He was so worried that his back would go again that he'd just turn around when it felt right and bowl. Flintoff is very envious of other fast bowlers who seem to be able to lope in without much effort and ping the ball down at ninety miles an hour. He is particularly impressed by the easy grace of his close friend, Steve Harmison, who always had the basic raw materials of a fast bowler, despite the need for the fine tuning that has now made him into an outstanding performer.

'But with me, there's a lot of huffing and puffing and strenuous effort that takes a lot out of me. But just imagine, as I carry on battling with my action after all these years of top-class coaching what I must have looked like when I tried to bowl fast as a youngster. Awful!'

But his batting was a major consolation as he settled into adult cricket. When Freddie was 13, he stepped up several grades and went off to join his brother to play league cricket at St Anne's. Blackpool Cricket Club was keen to take him on, but competition there was very strong and there was no guarantee of him actually getting a game. In his first game for St Anne's, his 30 not out helped secure victory and by the time he was 14, he was opening the batting for the first team. Around that time, he made what is still the highest score of his life – 232 not out for St Anne's Under-15s against Fordham Broughton.

'It was a 20-overs-a-side game, played on an artificial wicket and I remember getting dropped when I'd scored just six. My opening partner, David Fielding, scored 60 not out and we got 319 for 0 in those 20 overs. You don't forget days like that, whatever the standard you're playing in.'

So Flintoff was known for his powerful batting in and around the Preston area long before he fetched up at Old Trafford and impressed hard-nosed professionals immediately. His two cricketing heroes in his teens were Ian Botham and Viv

Richards, for obvious reasons. Flintoff was much taken with Botham's charisma on the field, the hex he appeared to have over the Australians, his attacking inclinations with both bat and ball, and his spectacular catching. Above all, he loved the way Botham won games almost single-handedly. But Richards was even more dynamic to the impressionable Flintoff.

'Every other batsman wore a helmet against the quicks, but not Viv. That

Getting some batting tips while with England Under-19s from Micky Stewart, the former England coach.

must have taken some bottle, especially as he played Test cricket till his late thirties. He also seemed such a cool guy on the field, sauntering around in complete control. He belonged out there against the best players in the world and didn't care who he upset. To a young lad, that arrogance was brilliant.' Young Freddie had a touch of that arrogance at the crease, even though he remained shy, keeping his head down, listening respectfully to his coaches.

He seemed to blossom with a bat in his hand, shedding himself of his reserve, appearing physically daunting rather than his usual gangly self when his pads were off. Lancashire clearly had him earmarked for greater things, noting the ambition that had taken him from Dutton Forshaw to St Anne's at a tender age. He went through all the appropriate age-group sides with Lancashire, playing alongside Mark Chilton, who has become a fine county batsman and Phil Neville, better known these days as a Manchester United and England footballer. But as Flintoff recalls, Neville was an outstanding young cricketer.

> 'Phil would open the batting with Mark, I'd come in at number four and then Phil would bowl them out for a pastime. The rest of the team didn't do a great deal. Phil played for Lancashire Seconds when he was 15 and I'm certain he could have made it to the top level. I suppose the chance of earning slightly more money than at cricket's other Old Trafford might just have swung it for him!'

Flintoff was also 15 when he made his 2nd XI debut for Lancashire. He didn't get much time to mull it over. After playing for the Under-15s against Yorkshire, he was asked by one of the coaches if he fancied a game for the Seconds the next day at Old Trafford against Glamorgan. He blurted out, 'I'll ask my dad' and to this day he doesn't know why he said that. Probably through shyness.

> 'Dad was chuffed to bits but I was bricking it, to be honest. I'd played against some fairly sharp bowlers in the league but I wasn't prepared for the overall increase in pace when I batted against Glamorgan. In those days the Old Trafford wickets were lightning quick and with the pavilion positioned sideways-on, you get a distorted picture of just how fast the bowlers were. The wicket-keeper was standing so far back, and then it dawned on me that I didn't have a helmet. I borrowed one and went out to join Peter Martin. Straight away, I copped a bouncer and managed to get out of the way just in time. Peter said to me, "You'll get a few more like that" and I did.'

But he played capably for his 26 and 13 in the match, although the soft manner of his dismissals sounds familiar to all Flintoff-watchers. He was caught at extra cover, trying to hit the medium-pacer Steve Bastien over the top, then the off-spinner Robert Croft had him caught behind as he tried to nudge him away

NEIL FAIRBROTHER
Lancashire team-mate

'He was very shy and quiet, but not in the nets when he was batting against the senior pros. You'd immediately take notice of his power and timing, even though he was a skinny lad. His bowling certainly didn't stand out in those days – his run up was awful, he'd start from anywhere. It was the batting potential we all noticed.'

down the legside. Flintoff was annoyed at those two dismissals, because he felt he had got himself out, rather than the opposition's merits doing for him, but he loved the experience and hadn't felt outclassed. He'd come to terms with the extra speed of the bowling after initial misgivings and felt encouraged by meeting the challenge head-on. That match made him start to think about a career in professional cricket. His team-mates had been paid for playing against Glamorgan, so why shouldn't he? But he was only 15 and hardly flushed with self-confidence. Was he up to the challenge?

Bowling for England Under-19s against Zimbabwe. I was never quite sure in those days if my back would go again, so every day when I bowled was a bonus. So this is quite a rare picture from my Under-19s phase.

Luckily for him, one influential man at Old Trafford had no doubts. David Lloyd became the first consistent mentor to Flintoff in his career and, since that time, has never wavered in his conviction that Flintoff was a special cricketer. The statistics may have tested Lloyd's conviction at times, as Flintoff exasperated so many of his admirers, but Lloyd has stood firm. His judgement of what it takes to become an outstanding cricketer shouldn't be queried. Known throughout the cricketing world as 'Bumble', he was an Old Trafford legend when Flintoff first walked diffidently onto the turf. Lloyd had captained Lancashire, was a good enough batsman to score a double hundred for England, had been a first-class umpire for a couple of seasons and was now the Lancashire coach. He knew just a little about the game, as he was to prove subsequently in his broadcasting career after finishing as England coach. A fiery character, the foot would occasionally stray into the mouth, but his players loved him because he would back them to the hilt – particularly younger players with much still to prove, like Andrew Flintoff.

Lloyd vividly remembers the day when he was convinced that Flintoff had that little bit extra. And he did it by scoring nought. 'I'd heard a lot about Freddie via our coaching network and I went to see him opening the batting for St Anne's against Preston. Malcolm Marshall was Preston's professional that year and he opened the bowling against the 15-year-old Flintoff. The poor lad was petrified because he knew why I was there. So there was extra pressure on him, quite apart from facing Marshall. Anyway, Marshall bowled him fifth ball, but it remains the best nought I've ever seen. He had time to play and looked composed against a great fast bowler – at the age of 15! I'd seen enough.'

David Lloyd went straight around to the Flintoff household and launched in with his Lancashire sales pitch. Over tea and biscuits in the front room, reserved for special occasions, Mr and Mrs Flintoff were given a rosy picture about Andrew's potential and the exciting prospect of playing for his home county. The Lloyd oratory that has become so familiar to millions of cricket lovers didn't really need to slip into overdrive. He was talking to Lancastrians who cherished the prospect of their lad playing for the county. Although Lloyd was all set to sign Andrew, there was a slight complication. Northants were also after his signature, due to someone at St Anne's doing some persuasive work. Believing that Northants were acting in an underhand fashion, not going through the proper procedures, Lloyd told Flintoff, 'I'll take you to Northampton and show you their facilities. Then you compare them to Old Trafford and tell me which club you prefer.' Game, set and match to Bumble, and Freddie told him he wanted to play for Lancashire. There was another consideration that swayed him. Northants had told him that he could go to Oundle School and study for his 'A' Levels while playing for them.

On tour in Zimbabwe with England Under-19s.

'They shot themselves in the foot with that suggestion! But there was never a contest between the two counties in my eyes. I was flattered that Bumble saw something in me and proud to accept the Lancashire contract.'

He was given an initial two-year contract, but after scoring a hundred for the Seconds at Liverpool, he was handed another year. The back was still a problem, so he didn't bowl in the games. His batting progressed, though, with the coaching staff amazed at the power he generated from what was still a thin physique. He won a regional award from the *Daily Telegraph* and it was presented by Ronnie Irani, at the time on the Lancashire staff, and later to be an England team-mate. An England Schools tour to South Africa at the age of 15 started Flintoff's regular annual cycle of England tours.

Flintoff was lucky to join a Lancashire playing staff that was chockfull of accomplished international players who were also collaborative team-mates, willing to pass on their knowledge to youngsters like him. He would sit in the dressing-room, only speaking when anyone talked directly to him and just listened to the likes of Wasim Akram, Mike Atherton, Mike Watkinson, John Crawley and Neil Fairbrother. It was a hard dressing-room, used to winning one-day trophies and tilting at the championship. High standards of professionalism were expected and no one was spared, no matter how illustrious, if those values slipped at any stage. But the disagreements stayed in-house and those players were friends as well as team-mates. It was the ideal training area for someone like Flintoff, who needed to be tested out on a more demanding stage than the ones he had dominated in recent years. And he knew it. He remains particularly grateful to Neil Fairbrother, a superb batsman with a remarkable record in one-day cricket.

'He took me under his wing early on, giving me so much guidance both about cricket and getting me used to becoming a professional sportsman. I'll be the first to admit that it took some time for the penny to drop about having the right professional attitude. I've always enjoyed a laugh and the social side of cricket, and I'm indebted to Neil for having such a caring, supportive shoulder to lean on.'

Fairbrother continues to have a major influence on Flintoff, even though he retired in 2002. He is now his manager under the International Sports Management umbrella, still handing out the necessary hard words about cricket as well as sorting out the various business complications involved in being an international sportsman.

Fairbrother was soon one of Flintoff's most vocal supporters, pushing for him to be given a chance in the first team. After scoring a couple of centuries for the Seconds in the 1995 season, he was finally picked for just one match. John Crawley and Mike Atherton were away on England duty in late August, so

Captain of England Under-19s at Southampton against Zimbabwe in 1997. To my right is the late Ben Hollioake, Alex Tudor is in the middle of the back row and Chris Read is second right in the back row.

Flintoff made his county debut at Portsmouth against Hampshire. It was not an auspicious occasion for him. Heath Streak, who became an outstanding fast bowler for Zimbabwe, dismissed him twice, for seven and nought. But it was Flintoff's fielding lapses that have stuck in the memory of the Lancashire players and their coach that day.

Mike Atherton wasn't even at the match, but still dines out on the three 'easy' slip catches dropped by Flintoff on the first morning. Neil Fairbrother is equally convinced of that tally, because he stood alongside Flintoff as the chances were spilled. The central figure swears it was just one. But he admits it was an embarrassing experience. It was all David Lloyd's fault. He had contin-

ALEX TUDOR

team-mate on England Schools tour to South Africa in 1993

'When he was eleven, Freddie was a tearaway fast bowler and no one wanted to bat against him. But when we were 15, in South Africa, he couldn't bowl because of his bad back. He only got on the tour because Ben Hollioake wasn't released by Millfield School. I couldn't believe they hadn't picked Freddie in the first place, but he ended up our top run scorer. I remember him blitzing 130-odd at Newlands; they couldn't bowl at him.'

ued lauding Flintoff to the skies all summer and the old sweats in the senior section of the Lancashire dressing-room looked sceptically at Flintoff's figures for the Seconds and wondered if the coach had been out in the sun rather too long.

On that first morning against Hampshire, Lloyd marched even further into the long grasses of hyperbole. He told the other players that Andrew Flintoff was the best slip fielder he had ever seen and must be put in that key position straight away. It was a very quick wicket and Wasim Akram, one of the world's great fast bowlers, was pawing the ground, waiting to get at the Hampshire batsmen. So Flintoff was duly put in at second slip, right from the off, when he should have been patrolling the covers or under the helmet at short leg, the traditional short-straw position for the tyro of the side. It's safe to say that after Lloyd's ringing endorsement, his young charge was under a degree of pressure on his county debut.

Flintoff, all those years later, remains keen to deconstruct the legend fostered by his gleeful friends.

'It was the fastest pitch I'd ever seen and Wasim was swinging the ball against two left-handers at a rapid pace. The first edge came to me early on and it hit me smack on the chest before I could move a muscle. Then a couple of half chances came to me that I got nowhere near. Wasim, who was captaining the side and desperate for us to keep winning as we chased the championship, was not impressed. He stood there, tossing his hair back, cursing and wondering what I was doing in the slips. Can't say I blamed him for thinking that, especially as Bumble told him I could catch pigeons.'

Soon Flintoff was moved tactfully out of the slips and Wasim continued to

Joining in the chorus of appeals with Alex Morris (second right) and Matthew Wood (right) during the second Test versus Zimbabwe Under-19s in Harare, 1997.

bowl magnificently, taking ten wickets in the match to set up a comfortable victory. But Flintoff had a vivid reminder of his nightmare morning. At close of play, he peeled off his shirt to reveal some massive bruises on his chest where the ball had hit him. According to his team-mates, there were three of them, of varying shades, while the man himself says there could only have been one because he didn't even stop the ball for the half chances. The exact truth can be left for cricket historians to unearth, but the reality is that Flintoff is convinced that Atherton and Fairbrother's grasp of facts has been sadly dulled down the years – not to mention the coach, who remains firmly in the Atherton/Fairbrother camp on this one.

After that game, Flintoff didn't play another championship match until 1997. 'It was a hard school at Old Trafford and I had no complaints about that, but it was back to the drawing board for me.' There had been another significant event just before Flintoff's championship debut. He played his first Sunday League match, at Old Trafford against Yorkshire. He was out cheaply, to Chris Silverwood, but more relevantly his back went again and he couldn't bowl. That was a constant worry for him in those days and did little for his confidence because he realised he had to be offering Lancashire an extra dimension, rather than just his erratic batting. He now admits, 'The gap between league cricket and the county version looked huge to me in my early years at Lancashire. I had no reason for thinking that I could bridge that gap.' That uncertainty was to last for some time.

CHAPTER 2

Marking Time

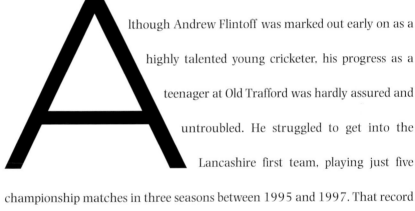

Although Andrew Flintoff was marked out early on as a highly talented young cricketer, his progress as a teenager at Old Trafford was hardly assured and untroubled. He struggled to get into the Lancashire first team, playing just five championship matches in three seasons between 1995 and 1997. That record made his full England debut the following year at the age of just 20 even more surprising in retrospect.

There were various reasons why Flintoff didn't storm into the 1st XI and nail down a place for the foreseeable future. Competition for places was very intense, as Lancashire kept falling just short of landing the championship after decades of striving. Flintoff wasn't showing enough consistency with the bat and his back continued to check his progress towards being an all-rounder, because he couldn't bowl much. He didn't believe he deserved a run in the first team, ahead of older, less naïve players.

Smashing a six when captaining England at Southampton against Zimbabwe Under-19s in 1997.

'I was in awe of my seniors in those days at Old Trafford. It was great fun in the Seconds, having a laugh with lads the same age as me, but I looked up to the top international players in the first team and barely said a word to them. I knew I'd done hardly anything in the game and didn't want to appear as if I thought I'd made it. These days, I do get startled sometimes when I hear young lads sounding off in the dressing-room after being on the staff about five minutes. Perhaps I've turned into an old fart!'

But Flintoff was popular in the Old Trafford dressing-room, despite the continuing advocacy of his coach David Lloyd, which could have turned counter-productive if players thought he was being unduly favoured. Young Freddie picked up some street cred with the seniors on a pre-season tour to Jamaica. He'd been his usual quiet self among the top players for most of that tour until one morning, en route for net practice in the team bus, Mike Atherton asked if anyone fancied a game of chess. Flintoff was bored and surprised the Cambridge graduate in ancient history by saying he was up for it. Flintoff may have appeared an unlikely adversary for the cerebral Atherton, but he kept quiet that he'd played chess for Lancashire Schools. His brother Chris had represented England Schools, so the talent ran in the family.

'I'd played at school from the age of ten. I was a bit of a maverick, going with my instincts. I didn't believe in waiting and waiting, plotting several moves ahead, then pressing my clock. Not much thought was involved, but I knew the moves and how to play it'.

Flintoff had kept such prowess under a fairly thick bushel, as you do when surrounded by tough, gnarled international cricketers. But that day he beat Atherton, much to the amusement of everyone on that bus.

'Perhaps Athers thought I was some oik from Preston pulling his leg. The bus kept careering round tight bends at speed and I had to throw up a couple of times out of the back window, then return to my game. Athers wasn't too pleased to come second to the shy lad and he hasn't asked for a game since.'

Another incident on tour that involved Flintoff is still spoken about with glee. It demonstrates Flintoff's gift of comic timing and ability to keep a straight face when necessary. Lancashire had gone on a 'jolly' to Jersey at the end of a season, to play a spot of cricket and golf, sink a few beers and enjoy a few laughs before the reality of winter set in. The opposition comprised current county cricketers, including that fine pace bowler from Hampshire, Cardigan Connor. Flintoff opened the batting for Lancashire, determined to play a few shots until Connor pole-axed him with a delivery that hit him in the privates – or the solar plexus area, as various commentators have described it down the years. It hurt and Flintoff came off the field, eyes watering.

Coach David Lloyd produced a pint glass full of iced water and told Flintoff, 'Stick 'em in there, Freddie. Freezing 'em will dull the pain.' The gauche teenager,

I don't play all that often these days, but I used to play a bit of chess as a boy. The England lads don't believe me, but I did represent Lancashire Schools at chess and – although he doesn't like to be reminded of it – I beat Mike Atherton once. And he's never asked for a game since!

DAVID LLOYD

Lancashire then England coach

'When you saw him stripped off as a teenager, you'd see a child's body on one side and that of a fully-developed bloke on the other. You needed them both to be the same, to ease the pressure on his back. His various injuries frustrated him so much. They stopped him growing into the Lancashire and the England team for a long time.'

aware that Lloyd was a tremendous practical joker, gave him a quizzical look, while the others looked on gleefully. He decided to take his advice and dangled his sore testicles in the pint pot, wincing at the cold. After a time, the pain subsided and Flintoff left the receptacle alongside his kit in his customary ramshackle manner.

Enter Gary Yates, Lancashire's off-spinner and one of the most dedicated professionals around. For reasons best known to himself, Yates had just had a hard net session at the end of the season. The point of that was not immediately obvious to his team-mates. He came into the dressing-room, wreathed in sweat, gasping for a drink. He spotted the pint of water and said, 'Freddie, is that your drink?' Flintoff concurred, leaving out the crucial fact that his tackle had been in the glass a few minutes earlier. Flintoff takes up the story.

'Gaz asked if he could have a drink and I said yes. But he necked the lot. He didn't have a clue until one of the lads told him about it. He said to me, "Have you?" and I said, "Yeah, sorry Gaz", while trying to stop laughing. He's one of the nicest lads in the game but what was he doing netting on a jolly boys' trip in September?'

It was hard to be angry with Flintoff for very long because of his genial nature, but his developing social life and fondness for a few pranks rebounded on him when a new Lancashire coach replaced David Lloyd. After Lloyd had got the England job, Dav Whatmore eventually took over, with a high reputation after guiding Sri Lanka to the 1996 World Cup Trophy. Flintoff missed the encouragement and guidance of Lloyd, especially as Whatmore made it clear early on that he saw Flintoff as a disruptive influence, a dilettante when it came to cricket.

'Dav and I got off on the wrong foot as soon as he took over. Some of the fault lay with me. By then, I had started to come out of my shell after discovering alcohol and getting to know my team-mates better. I was gaining more self-confidence as a person around people that I now knew very well.'

On a pre-season tour to Cape Town, Flintoff went out on the town with his Lancashire team-mates and, after supping well and not too wisely, they all meandered back to the team hotel at seven o'clock in the morning. They sang a few football songs, made a bit of a noise and made it clear to all and sundry that they'd had a good time. It was just a bit of daftness, but no one was abused and there was no trouble or damage. Two hours later, Flintoff – displaying the recuperative qualities that have long been admired – was at the nets, along with some of the other miscreants. He went through all that was asked of him, while a couple of the other roisterers couldn't make it. One of them – Neil Fairbrother, a Lancashire legend – actually fell out of the van, still under the influence, and had to return promptly to bed. But he wasn't upbraided by the new coach. Flintoff's card was marked, though.

Leaving the slip catch to one of my great mentors in my early days at Old Trafford, Neil Fairbrother. I was only twenty at this stage, young to find myself in the slips.

'I got fingered by Dav. He barely spoke to me for the rest of the trip and for quite a while after we got back to Old Trafford. Clearly, he thought I was the ringleader and didn't want me anywhere near his first-team squad, so I kicked my heels in the Seconds for most of the time. Dav didn't know me very well then and didn't realise that I've always been very serious about my cricket. I

JOHN CRAWLEY
Lancashire team-mate

'Freddie didn't have it at all easy when he arrived at Old Trafford. Not just in terms of the strong competition for places, but it was also a physical challenge for him. When he was young and gangly, he did swing it away from the bat with a model action, but that's no use when your back's in two pieces. So he had to re-model his action, making sure his feet landed in a different position, making him more chest-on, so he didn't put any more pressure on his back. It's remarkable he built up his pace over the next few years. He's had to work for everything in his care'.

was just growing up in a man's world, that's all. Since then, I've got to know and like Dav, but that night out in Cape Town did me no favours at all.'

Flintoff's chronic back problems also set him back. On an England Under-19s tour to the West Indies in 1996, he bowled a hundred overs in a week because so few of the other bowlers were free of injury. The reaction to that workload on Flintoff's back sent him back to square one. With only his gifted but erratic batting to offer, first-team opportunities were very scarce, even taking into account the antipathy of the new Lancashire coach.

But a rare championship appearance in 1997 saw Flintoff make his maiden first-class century, against Hampshire at Southampton. His parents were there to see it. It was a typical Flintoff innings in retrospect – 117, with 94 of them in boundaries.

'It was a very good wicket, with a fast outfield and John Stephenson kept trying to bowl bouncers at me at medium pace. So I said "thanks very much" and he kept disappearing.'

But that hundred didn't cement a first-team place. After getting his first 'pair', at Derby, he found himself back in the Seconds, frustrated and feeling insecure. He was still only 19 but that frustration boiled over at Bradford, when Flintoff was playing well against Yorkshire Seconds.

'I'd got to 30-odd, playing properly, keeping the red mists at bay when Gareth Batty came on with his off-spinners. Trying to hit him over the top, I was caught at mid-off and stomped off, furious at myself.'

When he got back to the dressing-room he kicked his helmet and threw his gloves and bat away. He then thumped the wall with his right hand in rage and frustration. Then he went to the toilet to gather his thoughts. As he sat there, with his head in his hands, going through that avoidable dismissal, he looked down at his right hand. There was a massive egg shape on it and it was starting to throb very painfully. Now he was wondering how to explain that injury.

Flintoff went to hospital where it was confirmed that the hand was broken. Initially, he told the 2nd XI coach Peter Sleep that he'd picked up the injury while batting, but that night decided to front up to the tough Australian.

'Sleepy said to me "I didn't believe you anyway. I was waiting for you to tell me the truth, you . . . idiot!" So the hand was pinned, I was in plaster for three weeks and missed the rest of that '97 season. Not that I would have played for the first team again anyway that summer. Dav Whatmore didn't say a word to me – perhaps the incident had confirmed to him how daft I was – but when I bumped into David Lloyd, he came straight out with it: "Not very clever was it, Freddie?" No, Bumble it wasn't. But at least it showed how much I cared about getting better at my cricket, how down I was on myself. Throughout my career no one has been harder on me when I fail through my own fault.'

But Lloyd kept faith with Flintoff in his new capacity as England coach. Lloyd's influence was obvious as Flintoff went all over the world with first the England Under-19s then the 'A' team. He captained the Under-19s in England and in Pakistan and thrived on the experience and responsibility, forging friendships with the likes of Alex Tudor, Robert Key and Steve Harmison that endure to this day. Key, a funny, streetwise character, shared Flintoff's musical tastes and they both relished the quality of Frank Sinatra, at an age when their contemporaries were deafening the team room with the latest rap or hip-hop monstrosity. Key also introduced him to the film *Casablanca*, making Flintoff sit quiet – for once – and admire the subtle inter-play between Humphrey Bogard, Ingrid Bergman and Claude Rains. 'Why should I be bothered with a black-and-white movie that was over 50 years old? But Keysy was right: it's a fantastic film. You can watch it again and again.'

When Flintoff captained the Under-19s in Pakistan, he was particularly sensitive in his dealings with a young fast bowler who was away from England for the first time. Steve Harmison was desperately homesick and spent a lot of time with his captain, talking it through.

Frustrated by South Africa's Herschelle Gibbs in the 2003 Test series. But earlier in my career I'd taken out my frustrations on a dressing-room wall, breaking my hand. I was 19 and soon learned!

NEIL FAIRBROTHER

Lancashire team-mate

'I knew he had something special about him when he was just 19 and he bluffed out the Australian batsman, Matt Hayden. We were playing against Hampshire and we had a team meeting, trying to work out how we could dismiss Hayden. Freddie said he'd get under his skin at silly point. So our spinner, Gary Keedy, is bowling at Hayden and Freddie keeps saying, "This bloke's got hard hands, he's going to pop one up at me". Sure enough, Hayden got rattled, tried to hit Keedy out of the ground and hit one straight up in the air. Freddie claimed it, of course – but it took some bottle to pressurise such a powerful hitter from silly point.'

'A few of the senior players went to Dav Whatmore and pleaded with him to get Freddie in the first team with us. But Dav had given him a black mark for that Cape Town incident, even though he was no more guilty than a few of us. But there was no point in keeping him stewing in the Seconds, because he was obviously going to be a bloody good player.'

'I loved batting with Freddie. Give him the strike with a quick single, then wait for the fun to start. He would hit at least one boundary an over when going well, and all I had to do was have a chat at the end of it and tell him what I expected of him.'

'In the NatWest final at Lord's in '98, I noticed how he was loving the big stage at last. We were fielding at opposite sides to Derbyshire's danger man, Michael Slater. We both decided to have a go at Slats to see if we could ruffle him verbally, just like the Aussies always do. So there's Freddie, aged 20, letting Slats know that he was near him at backward point. Not sledging, just verbal aggression. Slats got himself out soon after, having been wound up by me and Freddie. That made me think that Freddie had arrived, he wasn't fazed at having a go at the opposition's best batsman in front of a full house.'

'Harmy didn't know anyone on that tour and it was my responsibility to try getting him through his homesickness. At least he was honest and open about it and hasn't hidden it since. All he's doing is saying in public what we all feel at times when you're on the other side of the world and a bit down. It happens to every cricketer.'

In the end, Harmison did go home from Pakistan, with his captain's blessing. But their close friendship grew from there. Flintoff wasn't at all surprised that Harmison was so outstanding in the Caribbean on the 2004 England tour.

My friendship with Steve Harmison dates back to Under-19s days with England on tour. Here we're celebrating England's win in the 2004 Barbados Test.

'With his natural assets as a fast bowler, he just needed the right sort of guidance and luck with injuries. He'll end up with 200 Test wickets and everyone will have forgotten the indifferent start he made to his international career. As I know from personal experience, it takes a long time to adjust to the special demands of Test cricket.'

Flintoff enjoyed the challenge of leading players of his own age, rather than fitting in quietly among all those established internationals at Old Trafford. When leading the Under-19s in Pakistan, he was happy to stand up and thank the various hosts on behalf of the England party who were all at the official functions. The management team of John Abrahams and Phil Neale stood back as the teenager spoke fluently and with humour.

'I thought it only right that the captain should do the necessary if the High Commissioner had given us some nice food and drink, when these were a bit scarce in Pakistan. Playing alongside adults from the age of about nine or ten meant that I could string a few words together, rather than just mumble. That may surprise a few!'

Those early England tours also toughened up Flintoff mentally. He gained the confidence to mix it verbally with the opposition if the psychological pressure was on. He may have remained in the background alongside his Lancashire seniors, but wouldn't back down on the field. On the Under-19s tour to the West Indies, Flintoff took a dislike to a batsman called Adrian Murphy. He clearly rated himself and in the cricketing parlance was 'a bit of a strutter'. In the game in Trinidad, Murphy was dismissed by Flintoff who gave him a 'send-off', pointing his way to the dressing-room, accompanied by a few words of encouragement, laced with Anglo-Saxon expletives. Flintoff is not usually an exponent of such a practice, believing it disrespectful, but this particular batsman had got under his skin. Murphy told him he'd see him later, down at the beach, where they'd sort this one out. Full of youthful

bravado, Flintoff replied, 'Fine – bring your mates along as well.' But Freddie wasn't that foolhardy.

'I was only full of it because our physio, Dean Conway, was standing beside me. Dean's a tough Welshman who'd played as a rugby prop forward to a high standard. He was the sort of bloke you'd go into the jungle with, a very sound insurance policy if you fancied giving out some lip to a guy you didn't like. He sorted out Adrian Murphy with a few choice words – thankfully!'

The following year, in Zimbabwe, Flintoff again handed out some lip to an opponent he thought had gone over the top. Craig Evans, a bustling medium-pacer was clearly nowhere near as fast as he thought and Flintoff was amused at Evans's chutzpah.

'He was strictly a medium-pace dobber, yet he had all his fielders on one side, as if he was a genuine quickie. He kept moaning when we hit him into the open spaces, with time to spare. He had played Test cricket and obviously felt he was too good for us and was just unlucky on the day. So when they batted,

Evans was stood on the boundary, next man in, chatting away to some of his mates, with a cigarette in his mouth. He strutted out to the middle, got out first ball and I shouted after him, "If you hurry up, you might catch the end of that fag!" I thought he'd asked for a bit of a serve.'

Those two incidents underline a serious point about Flintoff's approach to cricket. Although a spectacular player, he doesn't like to see cricketers showing off on the field. He has rarely given a 'send-off' to an opponent and then only when he feels that player has deserved to be singled out. The same with 'sledging', where a player tries to unsettle an opponent by mouthing off at them.

Two of my best catches at slip – on the right, to get Adrian Rollins of Derbyshire in the 1998 NatWest Final, then Chris Adams of Sussex. I was very pleased in particular with the one off Adams, because it was a slow wicket, I was standing quite close and it still came quickly off the bat.

Flintoff was upset when the South African Dewald Pretorius gave him a 'send-off' after dismissing him while playing for Durham. When it was Pretorius' turn to bat, he got the full verbal and physical treatment from Flintoff.

'I really let him have it. But it should be enough for the bowler just to get the guy out, then celebrate with your own team-mates. In some ways, you've lost the battle by doing something that's basically disrespectful. I don't want cricket to end up like football where nobody seems to have any time at all for an opponent on the pitch. Cheating by diving for fouls seems to be just a natural thing.'

By the start of the 1998 season, Andrew Flintoff was slowly developing along the lines first envisaged by David Lloyd, then hinted at in various fleeting cameos by Flintoff himself. The practical experience picked up on his England tours had been invaluable, especially his first 'A' tour to Kenya and Sri Lanka. The volatile political situation that led to several being killed by bomb blasts near to the matches in Sri Lanka tested the resolve of the

England players, as did the idiosyncratic umpiring. With the heat and humidity at times overpowering, an early flight home must have looked an attractive proposition, but under the mature and relaxed captaincy of Nick Knight, the squad hung together and got a great deal out of that tour. Flintoff feels that was an important tour for him.

> 'I was just 20, with very little experience of first-class cricket and it was about time I was being stretched. I batted well in Sri Lanka and the standard of the opposition was high, with players like Atapattu, Jayawardene, Arnold, Chandana, Tillekeratne and Samaraweera playing against us – all guys I came up against later on in Test cricket. We crammed a lot of learning into a few short weeks and that tour certainly made me a better cricketer.'

That extra confidence brought him the bonus of an extended run in both Lancashire's championship and one-day sides in 1998. He became a regular in the team that finished runners-up in the championship and won the NatWest Trophy and the Sunday League in the space of just 24 hours. Lancashire persevered with Flintoff at the top of the order in all forms of cricket, thanks in some part to the advocacy of the senior players who bent Dav Whatmore's ear about the tyro's potential. Although he averaged only 26 in the championship and bowled very little, Flintoff started to feel more at ease with himself in such an experienced, professional set-up. To his great surprise, he was also a Test player before the summer was out.

The England call came in late July after Flintoff had enjoyed a golden few weeks where everything about his batting seemed to fall into place and the ball disappeared into the crowd on a regular basis. First, he scored a hundred in the championship match at Northampton in a big partnership with John Crawley, a batsman Flintoff has always admired hugely.

> 'He is such an intelligent player, so calm and versatile on all wickets. I loved batting with him, because he would spot the times when I was getting het up, and not concentrating enough. A quiet word or a kick up the backside would make me take notice. An awesome batsman.'

So Flintoff was in good nick when he played at Old Trafford against Surrey and made history. In a run chase, he smashed 34 in an over off the bowling of Alex Tudor, a team-mate of his on junior England tours. With Tudor also sending down two no-balls in that over, conceding two runs each, the final tally was 38 – the most expensive over in first-class history, apart from a blatant contrivance with deliberate no-balls in New Zealand a decade earlier. Here, Tudor was definitely trying to get Flintoff out and win the match for Surrey.

Tudor was fired up and bowling quickly. He had dismissed Flintoff for nought in the first innings and, after a solid start engineered by Nathan Wood and John Crawley, Flintoff had a licence to climb in. The target was 253 to win at five an over and Flintoff's pyrotechnics made a nonsense of the Surrey declaration. He

Celebrating with my Lancashire team-mates on our balcony at Lord's, after winning the 1998 Nat-West Trophy. Next day, we won the Sunday League.

made 61 in 24 balls, getting out just before the target was reached, the over after he had clobbered Tudor with such gusto.

Flintoff missed the last ball of that over, losing the chance to pass Garry Sobers' and Ravi Shastri's record of hitting 36 in an over. But he knew nothing of such statistical landmarks.

'Never mind, we won the match. I couldn't believe it when I was told all about those statistics. If I was going to make a bit of history, at least I'd done it against a good mate who'd first played against me for London Schools against Lancashire Schools when we were both about nine.

'I hit three sixes off Tudes in that single over. Two went back over his head, slightly to the leg side and I hooked another. One streaky four went through my legs, but I reckon the other three fours were genuine shots. Tudes was certainly bending his back and the challenge was on. His two no-balls came as he tried for extra pace. I particularly enjoyed one short-arm jab off him that went for six. At the end of the over, I just shrugged my shoulders at him and grinned sheepishly. He hadn't bowled badly, I just backed myself and got lucky.'

Adam Hollioake, Surrey's captain, also a current England player, praised fulsomely the talent of these two young Englishmen, Tudor and Flintoff, predicting great things for them. It had been a Bothamesque innings and in the next match, Flintoff did it again. In yet another run chase, this time against Warwickshire, he made 70 off 95 balls, as Lancashire successfully chased a target of 336. He was involved in a productive stand with his mentor, Neil Fairbrother, and the target was reached with an over to spare.

'That was a fantastic education to see Neil Fairbrother at first-hand, negotiating a run chase. It was amazing how he kept rotating the strike, giving it back to me as he dabbed the ball into space and called instantly for the single. He kept on at me, telling me where I could get my runs and which

Bowling for Lancashire in 1998, the season I made my England debut.

areas to avoid. He just seemed to see situations earlier than the rest and suss out what was needed, without any fuss. He made it easy for me.'

Commendably modest of Flintoff, but whether he liked it or not, the bandwagon was now rolling to get him into the England team. He was more exercised by the fact that those two spectacular run-chases had been successful, and Lancashire were now on a roll, fancying themselves for that elusive championship. But Flintoff's clean hitting had been noted beyond the horizons of the reporters who faithfully attended championship games and had seen him implode in the past through rashness or faulty stroke selection. Those of influence were informed of the quality of his strokeplay against Surrey and Warwickshire. They noted that

ALEX TUDOR

Surrey fast bowler – on the end of the Flintoff barrage

'He played one amazing shot in that over, just flicking a ball of full length over mid-wicket for six. It was into the wind and it just sailed miles over the boundary. And with no effort it seemed. It was Freddie's day at the office, but I didn't bowl badly. It was controlled hitting, not slogging. The full face of the bat. A very destructive batsman. There's nothing worse for a fast bowler than to be smacked over your head with a clean stroke, and Freddie does that for a pastime.'

'When he captained the Under-19s in Pakistan, I was very impressed with the mature way he spoke at the functions. No notes, he ad-libbed a lot and was very popular with our hosts. We were all very proud of our captain. In one game on that tour I was being bombarded by rocks down on the boundary and Freddie firmly told the umpires he wasn't having that. He was all set to take us off and the umpires made the police go into the crowd and sort it out. The stadium was packed but Freddie wouldn't compromise. He was very authoritative, very impressive. He had the total respect of his players.'

South Africa led the Test series 1-0 with two still to play and that England's batsmen had been disappointingly passive so far against opposition that appeared more positive and integrated. Ian Botham had made an immediate impact in his Test debut against Australia at the age of 21, despite unexceptional county figures, so why not give this 20-year-old Preston lad a chance? The call for youth has a seductive appeal when those in possession seem burdened by the responsibility, desperate to stay in the side, above all other considerations.

Besides, it would be fun watching this burly tonker giving the South African bowlers some overdue welly. It wasn't to prove much fun for Andrew Flintoff, though.

CHAPTER 3

Reality Check

There's nothing wrong in playing for England at a tender age. David Gower, Ian Botham, Mike Atherton, Bob Willis, Len Hutton, Mike Gatting and Graham Gooch all made their Test debuts around their 21st birthday. Some – like Gatting, Gooch and Willis – went back to the school of county cricket to toughen up before they established themselves as England regulars. But the selectors did Andrew Flintoff no favours at all in giving him his first cap at the age of 20 years and eight months.

Bowling in my early days of Test cricket, in 1998.

He had played just 15 championship games for Lancashire when the call came. He was raw and full of potential, but hardly suited to the specialised atmosphere of what was developing into a fascinating, tight series against South Africa in 1998. Flintoff had no real notion of what constituted a Test cricketer when he played for the first time at Trent Bridge. He also hadn't a clue whether he had that crucial ingredient in him, that indefinable extra which sets a Test match player apart from the others by strength of temperament.

Putting an exciting young cricketer into the crucible of this sort of Test series was an attractive proposition to the selectors, who would be aware that it would play well with the media. A young player always gets the benefit of the doubt with the public, who invariably prefer callow potential to a familiar face who is trying to re-establish himself at the highest level. The taint of past failure isn't there yet. David Lloyd, now the England coach, felt vindicated in his continual support for Flintoff – in the face of unimpressive figures for Lancashire – and the young man's blistering recent assaults on the Surrey and Warwickshire bowlers suggested he'd at least stand up to Donald, Pollock and company. England needed some red-blooded aggression to get back in the series, so why not take a chance on Flintoff?

But there were other factors that conspired against a happy start to Flintoff's career. He had gone off the boil with the bat since his electrifying assaults a month earlier. It often happens that a batsman loses form in the period between posting impressive enough scores to attract the selectors' attention and his eventual debut. Flintoff was just the latest. It would have made more sense to recall his county colleague, John Crawley, who batted superbly all summer, but Flintoff's bowling was an extra dimension that was deemed important, even though he averaged just seven overs per championship match in 1998.

The chemistry in the England dressing-room that summer wasn't conducive to a young player giving of his best. It was such a close series, against unrelenting opposition, that some of the England players were undoubtedly looking after number one. Places were at stake for the rest of the series against South Africa; there was an Ashes tour to Australia coming up later that year and, in the previous Test at Old Trafford, the crowd gave England some deserved stick as they followed on. An heroic rearguard saved that match, keeping England in

DAVID LLOYD

England coach at Flintoff's England debut

'I'd always gone on about his potential and when the captain, Alec Stewart, raved about him, the chairman of selectors, David Graveney said, "Get him in." We went on a gut feeling.'

the series, but it was Dunkirk rather than Agincourt and the sporting public expected more than just existing in the bunker, dodging the howitzers launched by the peerless Allan Donald.

So the latest bright young thing wasn't going to be garlanded with ready assistance and welcoming advice when he joined that under-pressure group of England players. Flintoff knew none of them, apart from his Lancashire team-mate, Mike Atherton, who in any event always retreated into his own cocoon of concentration when it was his day to bat in a Test. Atherton took Flintoff out for dinner two nights before the first day at Trent Bridge, and brought along his great friend Angus Fraser for company. But once the serious action started, Flintoff was on his own. He was, of course, very proud to play for his country, but didn't really enjoy the experience of his first two Tests.

With England in South Africa in 1999, warpaint duly slapped on.

'It was such a strange experience to come into an England dressing-room at 20, not knowing anyone apart from Athers and the coach. So I reverted to being a shy lad who only spoke when anyone talked to me. The senior players were clearly under pressure, and it showed. A few of them were too wrapped up in their own game to do much for a youngster making his debut and I understood that. My first experience at Test level made me realise that not every dressing-room was like Lancashire's, where the senior guys help any young player who's made the first-team squad. Perhaps it had all come too early for me.'

It certainly looked like it. Flintoff's back problem flared up again in the nets and it looked as if he might have to pull out. But he recovered to bowl 23 unexceptional overs in the Test. He batted just once, making 17 in an uncomplicated, refreshing style before getting himself out to Jacques Kallis.

'I tried to smack him over extra cover, but was caught behind. At least I'd approached my first Test innings in a positive frame of mind. There was no point in trying to play differently to the way that had attracted the selectors in the first place.'

Flintoff didn't have to bat in the second innings as England cantered to win by eight wickets. He was glad not to be called on, because as he watched Atherton win an epic duel against brilliant, sustained fast bowling by Donald, he realised how short he still was of the relevant psychological and technical equipment needed to prosper as a Test cricketer. The nous and ability to survive against bowling of that class and speed can't be measured in the statistics of championship cricket. The selectors have to go on a hunch that a player has the right stuff in him; the imperturbability to handle pressure situations. Nasser Hussain and Atherton showed they had it in their vital stand of 152 that broke Donald's magnificent spirit to win the Trent Bridge Test, but it was a chastening experience for Flintoff to watch such durability at close quarters and wonder if he'd ever attain it.

In the next Test, at Leeds, England scraped home on a final day of remarkable tension that ended in euphoric scenes as South Africa pulled up just short. Flintoff made two noughts and bowled just 12 overs, so he joined in the victory celebrations rather sheepishly. He was badly sawn off in the first innings, though – given out, caught at short leg when the ball clearly came off his pad. Flintoff, rather bemused, thought he'd been given out lbw and wandered off, thinking it had been a bit high. It was a shocking decision in a match of questionable umpiring. In the second innings, he was sent packing by a snorter from Donald that saw him caught behind.

It was an inglorious start, then, to Flintoff's Test career: just 17 runs in three innings and one wicket in 35 overs. He had batted twice at number eight, as the night watchman Ian Salisbury had gone in ahead of him as protection. The physical durability at Leeds of Angus Fraser and Darren Gough, and the battling innings from Mark Butcher and Nasser Hussain, made Flintoff aware of how much he still had to learn.

'Watching these guys close up, and remembering how Athers and Nass had batted at Trent Bridge, brought home to me the mental demands of Test cricket and how it drains you. The gulf in ability between the county game and Test matches was enormous, but I was now aware of the psychological demands involved. To be honest, I wasn't ready yet.'

It was with a sense of relief that Flintoff returned to familiar, welcoming faces at Lancashire for the final month of the season. He was dropped for The Oval Test against Sri Lanka and never had a chance of going on the Ashes tour.

'On top of all that, I had my England cap pinched at Headingley. Playing for England was far more important than a piece of cloth, but it was still upsetting. I don't have any possessions from my England career, apart from a photo upstairs of my hundred at Lord's against South Africa in 2003. It's a bit in-yer-face to show you're an England player at home. People come round who have careers themselves, so what's so special about being a cricketer? It's a bit flash, I think.'

So, after a harsh introduction to Test cricket, Flintoff returned to learning his trade with the 'A' team, touring Zimbabwe and South Africa under the captaincy of Michael Vaughan. Flintoff topped the averages with 77 and batted

Dismissing Hansie Cronje in the Durban Test of 1999. The euphoria can be understood when you realise that was one of the flattest pitches I've ever played on and I bowled thirty overs in this innings.

with greater judgement than he'd shown before. He was very impressed with the captain.

'I'm not being wise after the event when I say that Vaughany showed obvious leadership qualities out there. He was quietly impressive, thoughtful about his cricket but ready for a laugh when the time was right. He lets you express yourself through your cricket.'

Vaughan discovered insights into Flintoff's personality on that tour that have brought long-term benefits. 'He was the star of the show, getting a stack of runs and he was a lively character off the field as well. That tour gave me an insight into the way that Freddie works and the best ways of getting what we all want out of him. He's just a fun-loving character who plays cricket in the same way.'

It would have been interesting to see how quickly Flintoff's Test career might

NEIL FAIRBROTHER

Lancashire team-mate and, later, manager

'When he came back to Lancashire after his pair in his second Test, he was a bit down. He joined us at Southampton for a couple of beers and dinner after driving down from Leeds and he perked up, glad to be back in the mix with his mates. Next day, he took one of the greatest catches I've ever seen

– running forward from deep backward square leg, scooping the ball up in front of him with his left hand. It was a fantastic moment for him as all his team-mates ran to him. Very emotional for Freddie.

'He found regular failure very hard to take. He seemed to be making the same mistakes with the bat time and again. It was slow progress in those years. At Durham, in the summer of 2000, he twice got out cheaply. He lay in the bath and I thought he was going to drown himself. He asked me what he was going to do to get some runs. Freddie still gets down over his failures, don't ever think he doesn't care.

'At the end of the 2001 season, when Chubby and I sat Freddie down in the Old Trafford dressing-room, we told him that someone of his talent wasn't going to be allowed to just fade away. He was nearly 24 and that could easily have happened to him. He hadn't played in a Test for 15 months. We gave him those home truths because we love him to bits and also out of frustration that he wasn't realising his potential.'

have blossomed if a sympathetic captain, like Michael Vaughan, from roughly the same age bracket had been in charge during those formative years. Certainly, younger players who have come into the England side seem to bed down easier under Vaughan's understated, thoughtful leadership compared with previous disciplinarians such as Hussain and Alec Stewart. Maybe it's just the age difference, but Flintoff has played his best cricket for England under Vaughan's captaincy.

Flintoff's good performances on that 'A' tour proved the springboard to getting him into the World Cup squad a few months later. Before that he'd made his one-day debut for England in Sharjah, making a bludgeoning fifty against Pakistan. He bowled economically, fielded brilliantly and made a good enough impression to nail down a World Cup place, but it was not to be an enjoyable experience.

He failed in the all-rounder's berth, making just 15 runs in two innings and not being particularly economical with the ball. England slumped out of the tournament in the preliminary stages without getting to the Super Sixes, on home pitches that ought to have suited them in early summer. It was a massive disappointment to home supporters and the senior players, who weren't expected to be around for the next World Cup. For those like Flintoff, it was all over in a flash, and an anti-climactic one at that. The day after England had been eliminated by India at Edgbaston, he was playing for Lancashire in a National League game at Leicester. There was no time for moping around.

At least he found some form for Lancashire that summer after the ignominy of the World Cup. A couple of blistering hundreds in the championship and one off 66 balls in the National League kept him in the England selectors' minds. It did him no harm that the one-day hundred was against Essex and the new captain, Nasser Hussain, had first-hand experience of Flintoff's range and power of strokeplay. He was selected for England's tour of South Africa – on potential, but at least he'd been given another chance after the disappointments of the previous summer.

Flintoff showed glimpses of his capabilities in that South African series, even though he didn't get past 42 in six Test innings. He broke a toe in the fourth Test at Cape Town and had to return home, missing the one-day series. But there were times when he showed the raw materials were there for a worthwhile Test career.

On the first morning of the first Test at Johannesburg, Flintoff came in at 34 for 5. The light was poor, the ball was seaming all over the place and Allan Donald's pace and swing, coupled with Shaun Pollock's accuracy and skill with the seam added up to a massive challenge. Michael Vaughan, a colleague a year earlier in the same country on an 'A' tour, was at the other end, batting calmly and capably. When Vaughan was out at 90 for 6, Flintoff was left with the tail, a demanding situation for someone of his inexperience.

'When I first came in, I clipped one off my legs off Donald to get off the mark and he snarled, "That's the last of your freebies." It was too! It was hard work. My first Test for 15 months and I'm up against Donald and Pollock in conditions ideal for them. I thought it best to play my natural game, because with those class bowlers around, they'd find a special one for me if I just tried to block it out. I hit some good boundaries and saw off Donald. But I was left with the tail when Vaughan was out and I didn't really know how to do that. Perhaps I subconsciously relaxed.'

It was Flintoff's undoing. Lance Klusener, a medium-pacer whose glares and oaths were more menacing than his one-dimensional bowling, tempted Flintoff and he nicked one to the keeper, out for 38. He was very annoyed, having done all the hard work. But he was top scorer and that innings showed a great deal of promise. It was the same in the second innings, as England tried to stave off heavy defeat. He made 36 and again got out limply when he could have consolidated.

'In that innings, I came up against the fastest spell of bowling I've ever faced. Alec Stewart was at the other end when I came in and he was really going for his shots against Donald, who was fired up. Stewie got Donald's dander up and it was a superb, attacking duel. One delivery flicked Stewie's collar as he went to hook it and he said to me, "That was quick!" I thought, "Cheers, Al – you're one of the best hookers in the world, you tell me it's quick and I haven't faced a ball yet! Wish me luck!"

'I decided to have a go at Donald, rather than let him intimidate me. I pulled one bouncer over mid-wicket and got a couple of runs, which didn't impress Donald at all. The next short ball was even faster. It hit me on the hand and I decided to start ducking from then on. A fabulous bowler, Donald – he never knew when he was beaten.'

But it was a moral victory for Flintoff when he saw Donald off that evening and again after his first spell next morning. That might explain why he was then caught and bowled off a leading edge from the spinner, Paul Adams, when normally he would have climbed into him. For the second time in the Test, he was eighth man out after seeing off the two most dangerous bowlers. 'I must have relaxed when I saw Donald take his sweater. Welcome back to Test cricket, I still had a lot to learn.'

It was the same in the next Test, at Port Elizabeth. Again, Flintoff was left in an unfamiliar situation, batting with the lower order. Batting with Andy Caddick, he made 42 out of 55 for the seventh wicket, then the red mists swirled over and he got himself out again.

'I thought I should now have a dip because there wasn't much to come. So I hit Pollock for four boundaries in one over. By now, I was really pumped up. Pollock did me with a crafty nip-backer at a slower pace in the same over. It

The Port Elizabeth Test of 1999 and South Africa's Shaun Pollock has just given me a painful lesson about controlling my adrenalin. I'd just hit 16 in this over, but then he did me with a slower delivery and bowled me. A very clever bowler, Pollock. My learning curve was very steep in those early days with England.

was crafty bowling, but I got my feet in a terrible tangle and it looked an awful dismissal. As I walked off, furious at myself, he just giggled. I thought Pollock was taking the piss out of me, but as I discovered later, that's the way he celebrates taking wickets. That dismissal showed my lack of experience and clear thinking. Sixteen runs in an over in a Test match against a top bowler should be enough for any batsman, shouldn't it?'

After Flintoff had calmed down in the dressing-room, Mike Atherton sidled up and said quietly, 'Your beans were going, weren't they?' – dressing-room jargon for the red mists descending. 'It wasn't a crap shot, Freddie, but it's strange what strokes you find yourself playing when you're ticking.' Atherton had spotted a familiar problem for Flintoff that still recurs: coping with the adrenalin surge, maintaining concentration, proper stroke selection.

He was given a practical demonstration of that in the next Test, at Durban, when Gary Kirsten's monumental innings of 275 lasted 878 minutes. Flintoff bowled 30 overs in that innings and, although totally frustrated by the dead pitch, acknowledges the merit of Kirsten's knock.

'He just refused to give it away, taking no chances, determined not to give us a sniff, and so keep them one up in the series. I really rated Kirsten in my short time in Test cricket. I know that he and I have been totally different batsmen in style and approach, but he's the kind of player that all young Test batsmen could learn from. He just wouldn't give it away, and played within his limitations no matter how hard it was in the middle.'

So Flintoff returned home early from South Africa, more aware of what was needed at the highest level, but still finding consistency elusive. He wasn't to know it, but the new management team of captain Nasser Hussain and coach Duncan Fletcher had sized up the younger players in that tour party and made judgements on them. Fletcher was particularly hot on punctuality, self-discipline and physical fitness. Coming from Zimbabwe, where sports acumen flourished in an ideal environment as long as it was allied to the desire for self-improvement, Fletcher was not a fan of the burgers and lager mentality among young English players. Andrew Flintoff was to be the first high-profile casualty of this new ascetic broom.

Yet Fletcher and Hussain still believed in Flintoff, aware of his massive potential and showed faith in him for the first three Tests of the 2000 season, two against Zimbabwe and then the first against the West Indies. But, although bowling quickly at last, he didn't take many wickets and kept getting out at the wrong time. He made a top score of just 16 (three times) in five innings. He had no complaints at being dropped, but by now Flintoff's self-confidence was alarmingly low.

The focus shifted away from his poor returns in Test cricket to his weight. It was open season on him, with one broadsheet correspondent writing, 'Let's face it, he's a porker.' Some tabloids dubbed him Freddie the Fat Boy, and that inevitably led to abuse from the boundary edge about his girth – almost invariably from blubbery, red-faced swillers of lager who couldn't see their feet when standing up.

> 'The whole issue about my weight became a nightmare. I agree I was overweight – at the end of the season, I was up to 19 stone. But my back was again giving me pain, after a lot of bowling by the middle of the summer, and I couldn't train properly. I was living the bachelor lifestyle in a Manchester flat, eating the wrong food, but I was naïve and only 22. It looked worse because I had to wear a corset to help my back and that only made me look even bigger.'

Flintoff missed an early game in the triangular one-day series after his back flared up. Then the issue of his weight really came to the fore. Anonymous quotes from the England camp started to appear in the papers, suggesting that the reason why Flintoff wasn't doing himself justice as an international cricketer was due to his lack of professionalism.

> 'That amazed me. It was right out of the loop because no one had taken me aside and spelt out to me what I should be doing. I lacked guidance. I was struggling with a bad back and poor form, and these damaging quotes without a name attached were hurtful.'

To this day, Flintoff doesn't know who orchestrated that whispering campaign against him. Fletcher was too unsophisticated and guarded at that stage in his dealings with the media, but other senior figures knew all about the black arts of unattributable quotes into influential ears. What is clear is that the inner England sanctum were frustrated by Flintoff and wanted to give him a well-timed boot up the rear. But he hasn't forgotten that whispering campaign, or that no one fronted up to him with their misgivings.

By the time he played at Old Trafford against Zimbabwe, his morale was very low. It may have been in front of his home crowd, but Flintoff's feelings weren't spared.

> 'I got abuse from the crowd as I fielded in the deep and it hurt. I felt everyone was watching me, an awful feeling, and I was self-conscious about my girdle making me look even bigger. People shouted out that I was just a fat slogger and would I like another burger.'

Fielding in the deep at Chester-le-Street during the one-day triangular series in the summer of 2000. A miserable time for me as I had to endure a lot of taunts about being too fat from spectators who were just a few yards from me, in the outfield. It was difficult at times to block it out.

England won that match easily, with Flintoff smashing a few to make 42 not out, and picking up the Man of the Match award. Facing the inevitable anodyne TV interview afterwards, he contented himself with a muttered, 'Yes, not bad for a fat lad' and left it that.

'I'd thought about what I wanted to say, but it wasn't one of my longer

For once, Darren Gough and I were having a serious chat at practice. It was at Old Trafford in 2000, and I was getting fed up about all the jibes over my weight. Goughy was being his usual down-to-earth self: ignore them!

interviews. I could have said all sorts of things, but decided to keep them to myself. But I filed a lot into my memory bank about a few people during that difficult period.

'My parents were particularly upset by all the damaging articles and the comments from the public that came afterwards, and I felt for them. I didn't know what to say to them. I was embarrassed, and so were my mates. They didn't know how to go about making me more cheerful, so we didn't talk about it, even though they'd read all the stuff.'

Then Flintoff's trusting, open nature brought him further unwitting grief. His agent, the aptly named 'Chubby' Chandler of ISM, rang him after a suitable period when Flintoff had kept his head down, saying nothing to the media. He said the *Sun* wanted to do a sympathetic piece on Flintoff, trying to portray him in a more favourable light. Flintoff wasn't keen but was talked round by his persuasive manager. Flintoff spent 20 minutes on the phone to the paper, putting his side of the story, stressing that he was going to get himself properly fit once his back problem was sorted out. The result was a knocking piece along the lines of Flintoff being heavier than Lennox Lewis, the World Heavyweight Boxing champion. That hardly helped Flintoff's rehabilitation in the eyes of the British sporting public, the implication being that he was fat and lazy and not switched on to his cricket.

'After that, I didn't leave the house for a couple of weeks, unless it was to play cricket. It was a horrible time because I felt everyone was looking at me and sniggering behind my back. I felt isolated and disappointed that no one from the England set up had taken the time or the trouble to spell things out to me. At the age of 22, do you really know how to conduct your career?'

Eventually, Flintoff went out for a night in Manchester with a friend, to try to cheer himself up. Lancashire were due to play next day, but he wasn't fit due to his bad back. After a quiet pint in a pub, he went on to the Press Club, where he was spotted around midnight.

'I wasn't drunk but that didn't stop the *Express* running a derogatory piece headlined "Flintoff Punch Drunk". The implication was that I was out on the lash, instead of getting ready to play the next day for Lancashire. Not a word was written about my back problem.'

For a few days after that, Flintoff wondered if professional cricket was worth the candle. He loved playing for Lancashire, with his mates, enjoying the banter and the challenges on the field, but did he need the aggravation that came with being in the public eye?

'Socially I'd grown up in the past year or so – as you do when you're that age and you've suddenly got a bit of spare cash – but I wasn't a drunken oaf. I've always liked a harmless laugh and never looked for fisticuffs or aggro of any sort. That's just not in my nature.'

Soon he'd snapped out of his malaise and talked himself out of packing it in. He loved the game too much. He'd try to make some positive statements out on the pitch and headlines for his ability to play cricket, rather than sink pints.

That opportunity came soon after, on a sunlit afternoon at The Oval. It was a NatWest quarter-final against Surrey, the best team in the country that season. Lancashire needed 211 for victory and, after Alex Tudor had pinned Mike Atherton lbw for nought in the first over, Flintoff marched out. He clipped his first ball effortlessly through mid-wicket for four and proceeded to play wonderfully. Saqlain Mushtaq, at the time the world's best off-spinner, was played with consummate ease, while Ian Salisbury's leg-breaks were dismissed with disdain. Flintoff reached his hundred off just 88 balls and his undefeated 135 took just 111 balls. It was imperious, and Lancashire won with 14 overs to spare by eight wickets. David Gower, commentating on television, rhapsodised about Flintoff's batting. Everyone who saw it was of the same opinion – this lad could bat.

On my way to a match-winning hundred for Lancashire in the quarter-final of the NatWest Trophy against Surrey in the 2000 season. That was a difficult summer for me, with all the bad publicity about my weight and form for England, but that innings showed I could play a bit.

'Everything just clicked into place. All my team-mates had to sit in the same place in the dressing-room during my innings, and I was very touched how pleased they were for me when I came in at the end. Getting a lot of runs against the spinners was very satisfying, because it had been suggested in the media a fair amount that I couldn't play spin. Because the game was on television, this allowed cricket fans to judge whether I could play the game or not, irrespective of my weight. When I heard what David Gower had to say I was very grateful.'

But Flintoff knew he couldn't rely on his natural talent to progress: he had to lose weight and get fitter. First, his back needed surgery. He had an operation to numb the nerves at the bottom of his spine, but that didn't work. He was told not to bowl for the next six months, put on a special diet and advised about modifications in his bowling technique. To reduce the stress on his back, he was told to work on getting his front foot straighter down the wicket and getting his hips more in line. He would be more chest-on in his delivery, but at least that eventually eased the strain on his back.

Despite the damaging publicity of the summer and the obvious misgivings from the England hierarchy, Flintoff was picked for the one-day internationals on the tours to Pakistan and Sri Lanka. He would play only as a batsman. The all-rounder berth in the Test squad was denied him because he wouldn't be able to bowl and he hadn't made a credible enough case to be considered purely as a Test batsman.

His one-day performances that winter started off tremendously. England needed to get 300 to win in Karachi and, for the first time in their history, managed it. Flintoff made 84 off 60 balls and, for a short while, he became the darling of the media, a few months after being pilloried. But he wasn't taken in by that, nor by the innings itself.

'It was my day and I had any luck that was going, because the Pakistanis had to deal with the heavy dew, which meant it was difficult to grip the ball properly.

That made it impossible for their spinners, and the damp atmosphere meant that Waqar Younis and Wasim Akram couldn't reverse-swing the ball. So it was set up for the batters. I remember Wasim bowling me an accidental beamer which I pulled for six. It was either my head or the ball. A lot was made of my innings in the media, but in all honesty, their bowlers were severely hampered.'

Flintoff clocked up a few air miles that winter. As soon as the one-dayers ended in Pakistan, he flew home as he wasn't needed for the Test series. After a couple of days, he was summoned back as cover for the injured Michael Vaughan – purely as a batsman. David Graveney, the chairman of selectors, was on the same flight and when they arrived at the team hotel in Lahore, there was no bed for the player but one for the chairman. So Flintoff slept on the floor, the ideal way to cosset his suspect back after a long flight.

Next morning, he was in the nets, preparing for the Test next day, just in case. When the batsmen had finished, he asked the local net bowlers to stay

ALEX TUDOR

Surrey fast bowler who played against Flintoff
when he scored 135 not out off 111 balls, NatWest Trophy, 2000

'That was a high-class innings. He played Saqlain superbly and just took the game away from us with clean, controlled hitting. Against a good attack, he played some audacious shots, especially through the offside. Freddie never looked like getting out. I can't think of many better one-day innings.'

behind and give him some practice. The first ball broke his nose after he tried to hook a bouncer that went through the aperture in the helmet's grill. There was blood everywhere. This after being back in Pakistan for less than 24 hours. Were the gods trying to tell him something?

He wasn't needed in the Tests and remained unaware for a long time that Duncan Fletcher, in a press briefing out in Pakistan, had expressed doubts over Flintoff's long-term bowling prospects, due to his suspect back. The implication that the media drew from Fletcher was that Flintoff could only expect to be a Test player through his batting. This meant that he felt much work was needed by him, both in fitness terms and in technique and shot selection. It didn't sound an optimistic scenario.

Saurav Ganguly congratulates me on getting to my century at the Oval for Lancashire in the NatWest quarter-final of 2000.

At the start of the 2001 season, Flintoff had joked with his Lancashire team-mates that he'd probably have to take up off-spin to have any chance of getting back into the Test team. But a top score of just 42 in nine Tests hardly suggested that the batting stability was there – it was still a maddening wait for his undoubted potential to be realised. He marked time again in the 2001 summer, failing to make enough consistent runs for Lancashire even to be considered for selection against Australia. He agreed that at the moment he wasn't good enough to play in an Ashes series.

Flintoff was at a crossroads in his career. Lancashire had continued to show faith, batting him at number three, encouraging him to play long innings. But he couldn't manage that. He'd struggle against the new ball, get established then get out for 20s and 30s when the going was easier. He was clean bowled too often. Just two 50s in 22 championship innings added up to failure for someone of Flintoff's abilities. His only consolation was that his bowling picked up encouragingly. As the season wore on, his pace developed and he was relieved to make batsmen hop around as he hit the seam regularly. Perhaps he could get back in the Test side as an all-rounder, after all – if he could only show some consistency with the bat.

But he was nowhere near a recall to the England side and didn't deserve to be called up for the tours that winter to India and New Zealand. However, a phone call that September was to change his career. The penny was about to drop with a large clang.

Neil Fairbrother, for long Flintoff's mentor, had started to work for Chubby Chandler as his illustrious cricket career wound down. Chandler knew that Flintoff was neither maximising his huge potential as a cricketer nor his wider appeal as a sports personality. Chandler, who also handled the golfers Darren Clarke and Lee Westwood, hardly sylph-like figures themselves, had been comparatively relaxed about Flintoff's cavalier attitude to his weight problems. This was hardly surprising if you met Andrew 'Chubby' Chandler – the nickname wasn't an ironic one.

Horsing around after scoring a goal before nets in Pakistan, 2000. Some of us take football a little less seriously than the others.

Chandler knew that Flintoff admired his new recruit enormously, so there was a chance that he would react positively to a deserved rollicking. He deputed Fairbrother to summon his client to Old Trafford for a show-down meeting, what the marketing world calls 'a meeting without coffee'.

The three men met in the deserted dressing-room the day after the 2001 season ended. Fairbrother began in trenchant form. 'Look at the state of your gear,' he said and then pointed to John Crawley's kit alongside.

'He's the consummate professional who leaves nothing to chance while you give the impression that you can just saunter out and turn it on. You can't, Freddie. You've got to be better prepared. This is how a professional cricketer keeps his kit.'

Doing the drinks duties in the Lahore Test against Pakistan in 2000. I'd picked up that black eye in the nets on the eve of the Test, less than a day after I'd arrived back in the country. First ball. Welcome back!

Flintoff looked around his area and conceded that his team-mate had a point. The kit was just a mound, with pads, shirts, trousers and gloves sticking out at all angles. He neglected to point out that Mike Atherton's kit area throughout his superb career had been like that of a typical student, but kept his own counsel instead. This wasn't going to be a cosy chat.

For around 45 minutes, Chandler and Fairbrother lectured him about his lifestyle, diet and his attitude to fitness and cricket. They made it clear how frustrated they were with him, that his bachelor lifestyle, living in a flat with two mates, wasn't conducive to progressing with his fitness. Increased fitness and a more mature attitude to preparation would make him a better player.

'They accepted I loved cricket but queried if I had the necessary determination and professionalism to be an England regular. It was a firm statement of what they expected of me in the near future. They told me I had to stop fretting about who leaked all the stuff to the media about my weight, and just accept there was some justification for the criticism – no matter how badly it was handled. I was to stop looking for excuses, take a close look at myself and start to look forward. I took it from them, because I knew how much they cared about me, rather than just seeing me as a money-making exercise. Not that too many sponsors were keen on pushing deals my way at that time.'

Flintoff asked what he should do in the near future. That was progress – he knew he'd been told the truth, no matter how unpalatable it felt at the time. After a short one-day series in Zimbabwe, he wasn't due to report for one-day duty in India for another two months. Why not try to get enrolled in the new Academy of Cricket that had been set up under the direction of Rod Marsh? A tough character and once a great cricketer for Australia, Marsh would willingly trade home truths with any deluded young cricketer who wouldn't fancy hard work. But going over to the Academy in Adelaide would mean Flintoff would fill in time professionally. There wouldn't be much time for jolly socialising, because you had to be up at six o'clock every morning, getting fit to play cricket. Only then did the players see much of a bat and ball.

Flintoff agreed. He rang Duncan Fletcher, volunteering to go to the Academy at his own expense. 'Fletch agreed it was a good idea. He didn't say much, he rarely does but I sensed he thought I was doing the right thing.'

By September 2001, Flintoff was totally hacked off with all the jibes about his size and this meeting had been a necessary catalyst in an overdue change in his attitude to his profession. He had been hurt so many times by comments from the boundary edge.

'I used to get dog's abuse when fielding out in the deep. The image had stuck from the year before. They loved handing it out from the Western Terrace at Headingley – I was big and Lancastrian, so that meant double stick. I discovered that after you've played for England and got some publicity, those who want to abuse you hand it out even more. One day at Southampton I just wanted to drag one bloke over the fence and ask him what his problem was, because he just hammered me over after over. I like to banter with the crowd, but this bloke just stood there, swearing at me all the time. At times I could understand why Eric Cantona gave that supporter the kung-fu treatment after taking so much abuse. These drunks must have something missing from their lives to come to a cricket match, get tanked up and pick on a player they've heard about.'

But the best way to dilute the abuse was to give them less to jeer about. So the Academy sojourn, although very tough, was important. Flintoff got into a routine where he actually looked forward to the physical challenges, beating other players. There were no social distractions, though he would have preferred more emphasis on cricket techniques, getting different styles of coaching. At times he wondered if he would have been better off in Manchester, working hard in the gym and getting specialised coaching. 'But the most important thing was that I'd made a statement that I was trying to improve my approach to my career.'

It was noted by Fletcher. Within a few months, he'd be extolling Flintoff's virtues in a hotel in Mumbai, using him as an example of what can be done with dedication and the right attitude. Flintoff's Test career was about to be revived as well, courtesy of a slice of luck every sportsman needs. But it came at the right time. It was to prove the turning point.

In the Lancashire dressing-room at Old Trafford, where my business managers Chubby Chandler and Neil Fairbrother handed out some truths to me in 2001 that changed my attitude to my profession.

CHAPTER 4

Getting There

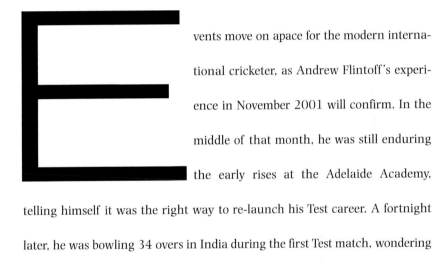

Events move on apace for the modern international cricketer, as Andrew Flintoff's experience in November 2001 will confirm. In the middle of that month, he was still enduring the early rises at the Adelaide Academy, telling himself it was the right way to re-launch his Test career. A fortnight later, he was bowling 34 overs in India during the first Test match, wondering if Sachin Tendulkar would ever play a false stroke.

Wellington, 2002, and I'm on my way to the second-fastest 50 by an England player in a Test match.

One of the few decent strokes I made in the 2001 Test series in India, when I had a nightmare with the bat.

Trying to get under the skin of Sourav Ganguly in the Test series in India in 2001. I failed, though. He's tough. Ganguly played a season of county cricket with us, but we felt he didn't get as involved in the team ethic as Wasim Akram or Muttiah Muralitharan. But, as I always say, there's good and bad in everyone!

Luck was the main ingredient in Flintoff's sudden return to the elite ranks. Within a week of arriving in India, the all-rounder Craig White had admitted to the management that his accumulated injuries meant he could no longer generate consistently the high pace that had disconcerted several Test batsmen in the past year. It was decided that he would stay as the senior all-rounder, because he could play the spinners well and could be relied on for reliable bowling spells, but he wouldn't be able to touch 90 miles an hour again.

There was a vacancy for the bang-it-in type bowler that Hussain and Fletcher felt might cause the Indian batsmen a few problems on slow wickets. The new ball would soon lose its shine, so that swing bowling wouldn't be all that effective and it would be naïve to assume that England's mundane spinners would trouble players of the quality of Rahul Dravid, Sachin Tendulkar and Saurav Ganguly. They needed to be bullied by the short ball, exposing their lack of height – or at the very least, kept quiet by disciplined, fast bowling that was just short of a length. England's bowling strategy was going to be attritional, aimed at boring the Indians out. But who could step into the breach caused by White's honest appraisal of his bowling?

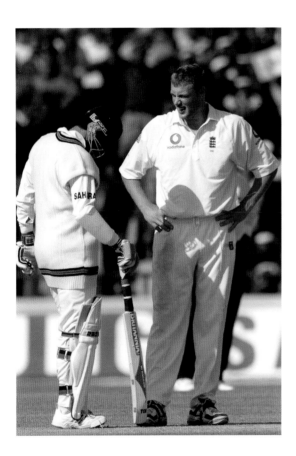

Flintoff's improved bowling for Lancashire – and consistent pace – hadn't gone unnoticed by the England management in the summer of 2001. They still had reservations about his professionalism and ambition, but not his heart, willingness to bowl long spells and his knack of keeping the scoring rate down. When encouraging reports filtered through from Adelaide about Flintoff's collaborative and positive attitude to his new training regime, the selectors decided to take a punt on him. He was summoned to India, took six cheap wickets and batted positively against India 'A' in his first game and was in for the first Test at Mohali the following week.

That started a sequence which finally cemented Flintoff's regular place in the Test side. Before the winter tours had finished, he had scored his maiden Test hundred, made decisive contributions to one-day victories in both India and New Zealand, and picked up a Man of the Match award for his bowling in a Test match. Even by the roller-coaster standards of Flintoff's career, it was a remarkable four months.

Ironically, it was Flintoff's bowling that cemented his Test place on the 2001 tour to India, after he had convinced himself earlier in the year that more consistency in his batting would be the only way back. He became a key component in the strategy of containment, conceding a miserly two runs an over throughout the series. Flintoff opened the bowling in the last two Tests and took 4 for 50 in Bangalore, winning the Man of the Match award. There was

The first Test at Lord's against India in 2002.
I'm glad I held my position here – if you fall away
in making this shot, it can be in the air too long.

nothing subtle about his strategy – just bang it in marginally short of a length, go around the wicket to the left-handers, try to tuck them up around the rib cage and disconcert them with surprising bounce. Flintoff's great strength allowed him to generate bounce, no matter how slow the surface. After bowling his heart out in the first Test at Mohali, taking nought for 80 off 34 overs, he was cheered by one message from a knowledgeable quarter. Angus Fraser, now a cricket writer, knew all about labouring long and hard for England on unresponsive surfaces abroad against top batsmen. On the third night of the Mohali Test, as Flintoff slurped water to combat dehydration in his hotel room, Fraser slipped a note under his door. He said that this was the best 'nought for' he'd seen in a Test. Flintoff appreciated that his old England team-mate had spotted the value of perseverance.

'I'd never taken my bowling in Test cricket all that seriously before. But here, I was bowling to a plan and managing to stay accurate while getting up a fair old head of steam on flat wickets. My dodgy back had hindered my progress and my chances of working on technical things in the nets, because I was never a hundred per cent certain that it would stand up to prolonged work. So it was a bonus if I got a bowl in a match. But in India, the hard work at the Academy had paid off and I enjoyed the responsibility of opening the bowling.'

It was just as well that Flintoff had suddenly become a key bowler, because his batting in the India Test series was shockingly inept. In five innings he scored 26 runs and it's hard to remember how he scraped even those together. He fell to the spinners on all five occasions through a mixture of tentativeness and gormlessness, an easy wicket for Anil Kumble and Harbhajan Singh. They'd been good enough to humble the strong Australian batting line-up earlier in the year on home pitches and Flintoff held no terrors for them.

'No matter how hard I practised with the local spinners, I was a sucker for Kumble in particular. Every time I came in, he was bowling and I wouldn't know where to get a run. The fielders seemed so close together, there were no gaps and those close-in seemed on top of my bat. I didn't have a clue.'

But Flintoff's breaking point came in the final Test at Bangalore when he was diddled out by the part-time offspinner, Sarandeep Singh, for nought. By now he was so leaden-footed, racked by doubts, that he just steered his fourth ball to mid wicket, instead of smashing it over the top, in the usual Flintoff fashion. Judged by haplessness, technical inadequacy and lack of concentration, it remains one of the worst noughts of Flintoff's career. And he knew it. In the dressing-room, oblivious to the consoling words of his team-mates, he was in tears. Aware that he didn't remotely resemble a number six Test match batsman, more a tail-ender, he was embarrassed and humiliated.

Solace was on hand, though, from a thoughtful man. Graham Dilley, a fine fast bowler in his prime, had suffered a lot in his professional career through injuries that curtailed his time in the game, then on a personal level through two broken marriages. Softly spoken yet incisive in his thoughts on cricket, he had impressed the England players on this tour as the bowling coach. Flintoff had certainly gained a lot from Dilley during many discussions. He was to glean even more now in Bangalore.

'Basically, Dill took pity on me. I'd gone outside, just to be alone, feeling very sorry for myself. Dill came looking for me and just chatted away. I can't remember what we talked about – it certainly wasn't cricket. Dill had been through a lot in his personal life and he could relate to my sense of despair. I shan't forget his kindness that day.'

After the India Test series, England played two batches of one-day internationals against India, then New Zealand. It proved a significant period in Flintoff's development as an international cricketer of substance. He learned to bat with the tail, eking out vital runs, instead of crashing on too early. His reliable bowling against India in the Tests had given him extra confidence and it spilled over into some influential performances as the team's premier all-rounder in the one-dayers. His role as a bowler was clearly defined – come on after the openers have had their spell, try to keep it tight and then bowl yorkers at the end of the innings when the slog was on.

All these ingredients came to the fore in an intensely dramatic match at Mumbai, when England scraped home by five runs to square the series at three-all. Flintoff also showed his flair for the big occasion and the unexpected at the end.

He'd already batted very maturely, nursing the tail to a total of 255 in 50 overs, coaxing Darren Gough along in a last-wicket stand of 37 that was to prove decisive. Flintoff was out for 40 in the final over, having a dip, but he and Gough had at least given the side a defendable total, with the asking rate at five an over.

But an Indian victory looked assured at 206 for 4. Panic then appeared in the ranks and spread as wickets fell regularly. Flintoff returned for his final burst and immediately got Harbhajan Singh caught off a skier. He was to bowl the last over, with six to win and two wickets left – the perfect scenario for a one-day match amid enormous tension, under the lights, in front of a capacity hysterical crowd.

Flintoff was more than equal to the demands. He ran out Anil Kumble with a deft piece of footwork, keeping his eye on the ball and side-footing it directly at the stumps. With two balls left, and six still needed, the experienced Javagal Srinath was on strike. Flintoff knew what was needed – a straight yorker – but checked that out with Darren Gough, fielding at mid-off, as he walked back to his mark. Gough, never short of a pithy response, came straight to the point:

Sourav Ganguly is dismissed by me in the Ahmedabad Test of 2001 and it's fair to say I'm pleased. Sourav didn't exactly fit in when he was Lancashire's overseas professional for a season and he has been a hard-nosed captain of his country since then. To be fair, he's also been a successful one.

'Leg stump yorker, knock the pole out.' Srinath heaved despairingly and the leg stump was knocked over. England had won gloriously, with Flintoff the man at the centre of it all.

At that moment of ecstasy, Flintoff metamorphosed into a footballer, intoxicated by success. He took off his shirt, waved it around his head like Excalibur, then set off around the playing area, pursued by his delighted team-mates. When they finally caught up with him, laughing hysterically, he continued to wave his blue England shirt around, as he imposingly dwarfed his colleagues. At the same time, picture desk editors on national newspapers thought, 'Thanks, Freddie – that's our picture. Hope our snap-

NEIL FAIRBROTHER
Flintoff's manager

'I thought that shirt-off thing in Mumbai was fantastic, but the tour management had a quiet word with him about it. The ECB marketing people missed a trick. They should have had that photograph on the front page of all their brochures for the following summer. It struck a chord with people who don't really follow cricket. Look at the joy on the faces of the rest of the England lads as they tried to catch up with Freddie that night. They didn't think he was being daft.'

per at the ground's got a good selection.' Freddie Flintoff had at last displayed in England colours the lust for life and laughter that had long endeared him to his Lancashire team-mates. For too long with England, he'd conformed, trying to do the right thing, inhibited by expectations then crushed by regular disappointments of his own making. His pores were at last fully opened that night in Mumbai and those joyous celebrations marked his liberation from the dull shackles of plodding conformity. No doubt, many lovers of the game back home in England shuddered at the exhibitionist nature of the euphoric scenes, wondering what cricket was coming to. Well, you really had to be there to appreciate what was involved and revel in Flintoff's uninhibited joy. He had been meandering along, in the inside lane of his career for a long time.

Batting with Graham Thorpe at Christchurch, 2002, when I scored my first Test century and our big stand helped set up victory. Thorpey is a fantastic player to bat with. He's so mentally strong and he rotates the strike cleverly. And he's in my ear when I lose it temporarily!

'I must have looked an absolute pillock. I'd watched Premiership footballers behave like that when they'd scored, just doing their job, and I'd think, "What an exhibitionist!" yet there I was, doing exactly the same. But in my defence, the atmosphere inside that stadium was fantastic, with firecrackers going off under the lights and we were so pumped up. We'd been 3-1 down in the series and squared it in the last over. Most of the crowd had come to see their local hero, Sachin Tendulkar, score a hundred and we'd spoiled the party. We refused to lie down; I'd played a major part in that victory and I was on an absolute high. That celebration definitely wasn't my style, it was just a mad few seconds. I look back on it now and feel embarrassed that a bit of flab was still evident when I took my shirt off. But I'd probably do it again in a similar situation – hopefully with a six pack around my stomach!'

Even the normally taciturn England coach Duncan Fletcher was moved by Flintoff's match-winning performance, if not by his unfettered delight. That night, as the England party prepared for an early morning flight to New Zealand, the coach sat in the café of the Taj Mahal Hotel, extolling Flintoff's willingness to buckle down and learn the hard way about international cricket. Clearly impressed by Flintoff volunteering to go to the Academy a few months earlier, he came as near as he ever will to waxing lyrical about the rewards available to England cricketers willing to do all that's necessary to maintain high standards. It was in graphic contrast to the briefing Fletcher had given the media in Pakistan a year earlier, when he had doubted whether Flintoff would be able to bowl enough to be a Test all-rounder.

Flintoff was just delighted to be making important contributions to England's matches, after so much frustration.

'I'd been totally focused since joining the boys in India. I wanted to better myself, I didn't need the big stick waved at me any more, or leaks to the media. After so much frustration I was starting to feel good about myself as an international cricketer, desperate to make up for so much lost time.'

He certainly did that in his next two Tests, in New Zealand. First came Flintoff's maiden Test century, at Christchurch. Typically, it came when he was on a 'pair', desperate to avoid a repetition of Headingley '98. But more relevantly, he helped England out of trouble to establish a winning platform. When he came out to join Graham Thorpe on 106 for 5, the lead was just 187 and with the pitch drying out after early moisture, something around 300 was the least England needed for security. Flintoff had been embarrassed by a top score of just 42 in 12 Tests and the memory of his palsied efforts in India was still fresh. After his duck in the first innings, his grisly tally was eight runs in the last five Test knocks. It's no understatement that it was time to deliver, otherwise he would slip further than seven down the batting order or even miss out altogether.

Fortunately, Thorpe was the ideal partner for Flintoff – unflappable, vastly experienced and a left-hander able to disrupt the bowlers' line alongside the right-handed Flintoff. The two, ostensibly opposites in temperament, had become close on those two winter tours. Thorpe's marriage breakdown and early departure from the Test leg of the Indian tour had been public and embarrassing for him, while Flintoff had also felt exposed due to his poor efforts with the bat.

'Thorpey knew all about despair and personal distractions and even though there were a few years between us, we could relate to what we'd gone through. He seems to be in your head, knowing what you're thinking before you do. We'd spent a fair amount of time together in Christchurch before that Test, chilling out over a game of pool and a few beers.'

Thorpe had told Flintoff to remain positive in defence as well as attack, to bristle with defiance and not appear as if he didn't belong in the Test-match arena. As soon as he came to the crease, with the match in the balance, Thorpe came up to him, punched him in the stomach and said 'Remember what I told you in the pub.' Straight away, Flintoff started to cream boundaries, getting to 26 off his first 13 deliveries, refusing to be cowed by the situation of the match. The two batsmen fed off each other and it was surprising during their partnership that the nudger and nurdler Thorpe kept pace with the more expansive Flintoff in personal scoring rates.

Flintoff had the inevitable rushes of blood along the way to his first Test hundred. He carved one six that could easily have been caught on the boundary and Thorpe was at him straight away. 'Come on!' he shouted. 'You've had all this time without a hundred! There'll be plenty of days when you can't lay a bat on it!' Thorpe was assessing the state of the game more clearly than his excited partner. The wicket was drying out to be a belter, so a big lead was vital and the New Zealanders had lost their best bowler, Chris Cairns, with a knee injury. A lead of more than 400 was now necessary.

Flintoff reached his hundred fortuitously, but at least by playing his natural game. The bustling medium-pacer Craig McMillan had been tempting him with a string of bouncers, trying to get him to mistime a hook or pull. Uncharacteristically, Flintoff was biding his time, ducking under them and ignoring McMillan's verbal byplay. Eventually, he reverted to type, told himself, 'The next one's got to go' and top-edged the inevitable bouncer over third man to go from 98 to 102. Hugs from Thorpe, a feeling of joy mixed with relief from Flintoff and a long stare at the scoreboard announcing he'd finally got there in a Test match.

'When we came into the dressing-room at the tea interval, the lads were absolutely buzzing. They said they wouldn't be changing their seats after tea, that we just had to keep going. Before we went out again, I started skipping

Graham Thorpe congratulates me on my maiden Test century, Christchurch, 2002.

up and down, which is definitely not like me. My Lancashire team-mate Warren Hegg noticed and said, "What are you doing, Freddie?" and I just grinned gormlessly and said, "I've got a Test-match hundred!" I couldn't stop laughing and grinning.'

He carried on thumping the ball with great gusto after tea, until holing out for 137, caught at deep mid-wicket, a Flintoffian area of dismissal. Thorpe made an unbeaten double hundred and the pair had established a new record for England for the sixth wicket of 281. With the lead now 551, that stand had put England firmly in command. They couldn't lose it now, could they?

Well, they would have done so if Nathan Astle had managed to stay at the crease a little longer. In an astonishing display of clean hitting, Astle made the fastest double hundred in terms of balls received and his 222 meant New Zealand fell just 98 runs short. All the England bowlers, including Flintoff, were hammered and all the talk afterwards was of Astle's withering assault, rather than the result. Flintoff agreed with Thorpe that Astle, not the Surrey left-hander, ought to have picked up the Man of the Match award.

'Funny how it rarely goes to someone on the losing side. Astle was absolutely amazing that day. And I thought I could hit the ball! But we'd won a Test with a day to spare, and I'd played a part in that. Next day, I celebrated long and hard with Thorpey and Mark Butcher in an Irish bar in Christchurch. Well, it was St Patrick's Day. Two good reasons to drink some Guinness!'

A week later, the England players were sitting in the bar of their hotel in Wellington, sharing a melancholy hour together, drowning their sorrows. Ben Hollioake had been killed earlier that day in a car crash in Perth, Western Australia. The same Ben Hollioake who had been with them during the recent one-day series in New Zealand, who then stayed on for a holiday with his girlfriend, meeting up with his England team-mates. Ben Hollioake played cricket with dreamy insouciance, making it look ridiculously easy at his best. His relaxed personality meant he was enormously popular among cricketers and, at the age of 24, he was bound to become a highly influential England cricketer.

It's not a competition, of course, but some of the England players in Welling-

Acknowledging the crowd's applause after I'd reached a rapid 50 against New Zealand in the Wellington Test of 2002. But the runs meant nothing to me – my good friend Ben Hollioake had just died in a car crash, which explains the black armband.

ton that day were particularly devastated by Ben's death. Andrew Flintoff was one of them.

'I'd known Ben from the age of eight and we'd played together through all the under-age England groups. Our backs had both played up on the same day, when making our debuts for England Under-15s. I couldn't believe it. I was padded up on the third morning, next man in, when I noticed that Mark

GRAHAM THORPE

Flintoff's England team-mate

'That hundred at Christchurch was vital for him. It helped Freddie work out what batting's all about in a Test match. Even when he played a rare defensive stroke, he enjoyed it. Robin Smith could hit the ball hard, but in my time, no English batsman has hit the ball harder straight down the ground. He can make the opposition look hopeless in the field.'

'His attitude on tour in 2001–02 was great at all times, even when he wasn't scoring runs in India. Everyone had been on his case two years earlier about his weight, but he remained upbeat. He's a gentle giant.'

Butcher and Graham Dilley were very upset. In all innocence I said to Warren Hegg, "What's up? Has someone died?" Warren told me to shut up and concentrate on the cricket, but eventually I found out after persisting.

'Ben had always appeared invincible to me – highly talented, laid back, smiling most of the time. That so relaxed a guy had died so violently was horrible. He was the first person that I'd known who had died young and that made us all think very hard over the next few weeks, thousands of miles from home.'

It mattered naught to Flintoff that two days after Ben's death, he battered a rapid 50 on the final morning of the Wellington Test. The declaration was nigh, he had been given licence to let fly and his 50 came off 33 balls. Only

Ian Botham among England players had surpassed that in making a Test-match 50. Flintoff went on to make 75 off 44 deliveries. 'But it didn't mean a thing to me. I just crashed it around and barely acknowledged the crowd's applause when I got 50, then out. There were more important things to consider.'

Ben Hollioake's sudden death knocked the stuffing out of that England party and Nasser Hussain had to work very hard on their morale for the rest of that tour. They lost the Auckland Test, not enjoying the best of fortune with toss, weather and umpiring decisions – including a shocker that saw Flintoff given out caught behind when nowhere near the ball. Even the bowler, Andre Adams looked sheepish when the decision went his way. But New Zealand squared the series when most good judges agreed that England were superior.

But Flintoff returned home a more fulfilled cricketer than he had been just a few months earlier. He had averaged 40 with the bat in the New Zealand Test series, bowled with spirit throughout the two tours and made significant con-

Since the end of 2001, I've had to get used to hours of this in the gym. But it's true: no pain, no gain!

tributions to several one-day internationals, especially when the pressure was on. Duncan Fletcher's gimlet eye had been trained on Jimmy Ormond and Usman Afzaal for defects in overall fitness while in New Zealand, with the inevitable media focus on them, and although Flintoff could sympathise with

the two players, he was glad the heat was off him in that department. Two hard Test series had toughened him up mentally; he was getting fitter and his performances were more consistent. When he left New Zealand, he weighed 16½ stone, compared to the 19 of just 18 months ago. And he'd been the one to seize the initiative after reality had finally dawned. Messrs Chandler and Fairbrother had acted productively for both English cricket and their client.

The importance of Flintoff to England was about to become apparent in the summer of 2002, with depressing implications for the player. Ahead lay an important year that included an Ashes tour to Australia and then the World Cup in Zimbabwe and South Africa. But, because of the selectors' short-sighted strategy, Flintoff could make only the World Cup – and then at the last gasp.

Flintoff picked up a groin injury early in June that just wouldn't go away. It ended up as a double hernia that required an operation in September. He was then in a race against time to get himself fit for the Ashes tour. If the selectors hadn't been so obsessed with winning the home Test series against India, they would have taken their top all-rounder out of the equation, ordered him to rest, then set in train the necessary surgery. He was, after all, on a central contract – the Holy Grail for Duncan Fletcher, which allowed him to supervise his players in all aspects. It still beggars belief that Flintoff was sent back over the top in two gruelling Tests before the injury flared up seriously. He bowled more overs in that Test series than any other England fast bowler apart from Matthew Hoggard, on top of batting at number six and being a key fielder. He was now precious cargo for England, yet handled like a willing workhorse. Flintoff was too accommodating to demur, but his treatment in 2002 was surely wrongly geared towards winning the Indian series. More concern could have been given to safeguarding the player's long-term welfare. Since Flintoff made his Test debut, he has missed all of the three Ashes series, for various reasons – the last one through selectorial dogma and pragmatism.

> 'I first tweaked my groin in the field when we played Warwickshire in the Benson and Hedges Cup semi-final. We lost a close game at the death and when that happens, you feel every aching bone in your body. Fast bowlers are never one hundred per cent because it's such an unnatural action. I'm also not exactly a supple athlete when I'm bowling, so I was bound to experience a few niggles in a busy season. I just hoped that niggle in my groin would go away over the next few days. It didn't.'

He got through the one-day triangular series, playing well, entertaining many, but still troubled by his groin. In the Trent Bridge Test, he sent down 49 overs on a flat pitch as England strained for victory on the last day which would have put them 2-0 up with two to play. We'll never know if Flintoff might have been rested for the remainder of that summer had India not held out, but he was wheeled out again for Headingley, where he bowled 27 overs when manifestly not fit. On top of that, he picked up another 'pair' in a Headingley Test. Afterwards, Hussain admitted that Flintoff should probably not have played, but the damage was done.

> 'I'd been pumped full of anti-inflammatories to get me through at Trent Bridge, but at times I couldn't lift my leg up. I definitely wasn't fit for Headingley and was hanging by a thread. But England had the final say on my fitness as a centrally contracted player, so I was in their hands.'

Headingley ended Fintoff's season in mid-August. Now it was a race to get him fit for the Ashes tour, starting in just two months' time. Surgery was needed on a bilateral inguinal disruption: a double hernia to the lay person. It was a small tear that widens, the kind of condition often suffered by professional foot-ballers. After the operation at the start of September, there was rehabilitation at the National Sports Centre at Lilleshall. There was no guarantee that Flintoff would be fit for Australia.

I'm looking at the hill I'm about to run up 30 times – much to the pleasure of my physio guru, Dave Roberts, February 2004.

When the party arrived in Australia at the end of October, Flintoff wasn't fit enough to run. The management despaired, but had they done their medical homework on a double hernia operation? Only a few years back, footballers regularly had to retire from such a long-term groin injury. It was the most serious one Flintoff had yet picked up in his career. Time and patience were needed, not the quick-fix attitude that had landed him in this state.

He was eventually packed off to the Academy in Adelaide to speed up the recovery process. 'I did start to pick up, but there are only so many alarm clocks going off at six o'clock you can take. You can do the physical work time after time, but you have to find out if you're match fit.'

He did in the match against Queensland that preceded the first Test. After bowling 28 overs in the game, it was clear that he was a long way off the required fitness. He was sent home with the aim of getting fit for the World Cup the following February. Another Ashes series had passed Andrew Flintoff by.

'When I was told I was going home, I was relieved. You don't stay on an Ashes tour unless you're fit and available to play. I clearly wasn't fit, through no fault of my own. A few ill-researched comments about me then flew about. Lord MacLaurin, who was about to retire as the Chairman of the ECB, said he couldn't understand why footballers could be fit within a month of my sort of operation, but Flintoff wasn't. So the implication was that I hadn't been doing my rehab properly. The image of lazy Freddie from the summer of 2000 was dusted off again and that really depressed me.

'Now Lord MacLaurin made a fortune out of reviving the Tesco supermarket chain and I'd never dream of telling him how much he should charge for a tin of baked beans, so why was he sticking his oar in? As I found

Putting in the hard work around the hills of Bolton. It was here the physiotherapist Dave Roberts worked me so hard while I recovered from my double hernia operation towards the end of 2002. One day off at Christmas!

out from the experts who treated me, those comparisons with footballers aren't valid. Not many of them are my height and weight, and the demands on fast bowlers are specific to that sport. If you ask a footballer to bowl six fast deliveries in a row, then stand around in the field and do it all over again a few minutes later, he'd struggle.'

When Flintoff had started his rehabilitation at Lilleshall, before going out to Australia, one of the doctors told him, 'I can guarantee you fitness for the one-day games in January in Australia, but nothing else. If you're fit enough to play in any of the Tests out there, that's a bonus.' Yet Flintoff was stuck in the middle, uncertain and being pilloried. 'The England camp was surprised that I was taking such a long time to recover, but the medical experts weren't. I was just doing as I was told, yet I was the one getting the stick in public.'

So when he returned from Australia, the Flintoff disposition was far from sunny. He needed his spirits revived at once so that his painful rehabilitation would start positively. He found the ideal man. Dave Roberts had been the physio on several England tours in the mid-nineties after working with Worcestershire, and he was now contracted for a certain amount of days with Lancashire during the season. Known as 'Rooster' because of his protruding nose, he is a genuine character with a vivid turn of phrase, unwilling to deal in platitudes when home truths have to be dispensed. Having played league cricket for Middleton in the Central Lancashire League, he knew enough about the pitfalls of professional cricket and his salty humour revived Flintoff's spirits.

'I rented a flat in Altrincham and settled down to endless days of training

DAVE ROBERTS

Physio during Flintoff's rehab

'That period was the turning point in his career for injuries and how to deal with them. It was the most serious one for him in terms of just what he had to do. Without that operation, his bowling would not have carried on. At last Freddie realised how fit he had to be to bowl fast consistently. He'd been letting himself down with his general fitness before that.'

under Rooster's supervision. He gave me Christmas Day off, which I spent on my own. My parents, hoping to see me play in the Melbourne Test, had booked a holiday in advance of my return and they'd met up there with my brother, who'd come over from Japan for the same reason. It wasn't a time to feel sorry for myself, though, the World Cup was too close for that.'

Dave Roberts' initial challenge was to rebuild Flintoff's confidence in the first few weeks. He warned him to expect a lot of pain. They spent up to five hours a day together – in the gym, the swimming pool, running up and down the hills by the side of a reservoir near Bolton. Roberts made it quite clear he was giving up a lot of his family time around Christmas and New Year, so he didn't expect to be mucked around. He got the response he was looking for from Flintoff.

'I didn't get near a cricket ball for a few weeks and by the time he'd finished with me, I'd lost a stone in weight and felt much stronger. The training was very hard but Rooster's an infectious person, with a great sense of humour, who drives you on. He's got an opinion on everything, so we talked about women, cars, finances, sport, life in general and we got on really well. The only thing that got to me was his constant memories of Ian Botham at Worcestershire! Half of them I didn't believe anyway.'

Roberts advised him to develop enough protective muscle structure to deal with vulnerable areas like the groin, spine and abdomen when they were under stress. He said that adjusting the bowling action to compensate for the weakness in Flintoff's back was a result of carrying too much weight in the past. So there'd been extra pressure on his groin because of his size and his style of bowling that required a lot of effort.

'I had this nagging doubt that I'd break down again in either the back or the groin, but Rooster was great at instilling confidence in me that I'd be fine as long as I kept up the training. He gave me a general circuit training programme that I've stuck to since, and the results are obvious. I've never felt fitter. So much is in the brain. Rooster told me that he used to spend 99 per cent of his time massaging Beefy Botham's brain and that the England physio Wayne Morton was the same with Darren Gough. After a time these players trusted their physio implicitly, and that was the same with me and Rooster. I reckon he got down from 99 per cent with me to 70 per cent as I took more responsibility.'

Those weeks spent with Dave Roberts would prove to be the most valuable yet in Andrew Flintoff's career, because it was spelt out to him in clear, plain language, laced with the occasional Anglo-Saxon expletive, just what was necessary to sustain an international career as an all-rounder. Flintoff drank it all in because he knew that Roberts was right. Yet even as he supervised the final training sessions, Roberts still insisted on the plain, unvarnished truth. He said he couldn't guarantee to Flintoff that he'd be fit for the World Cup. It would be a close call. Nothing ever seemed straightforward at that stage of Flintoff's life.

CHAPTER 5

A Memorable Year

A The year 2003 was the happiest yet of Andrew Flintoff's young life. Everything that was important to him appeared to gel beautifully. He was very fit, established at last as an England regular, with the figures to back that up. In eight Tests in 2003 he averaged 40 and took 19 wickets and, in one-day internationals, he averaged 45 with the bat and took 30 wickets. He would have taken even more Test wickets if he hadn't been very unlucky with dropped catches but, typical of his new serene philosophy, Flintoff didn't play up on the field or mope in the dressing-room.

'No one drops a catch on purpose and I know how difficult it can be, particularly in the slips. I've dropped a few there. It's more important that the guy knows you understand and hope he gets it right next time.'

The Lord's Test against South Africa when I broke my bat whacking one off Makhaya Ntini, on my way to a hundred.

One of the main reasons for Flintoff's serenity was that he'd got engaged to Rachael Wools. Working on the marketing side for the Test match sponsors, npower, Rachael knows just enough about cricket to relate to her fiance's ambitions, but is intelligent enough to let the subject drop when quality time is the aim.

'Rachael's got her own career. She's not living her life through mine and we talk very little about cricket when we're on our own. That suits me fine. I felt settled and content and that was reflected in my cricket.'

He also had to come to terms with a higher profile. As Flintoff's consistent performances and engaging personality brought him to the attention of a wider

MARK BUTCHER

England team-mate

'Freddie would rather get out being aggressive than poking around, and he's right to think that. That's not being irresponsible, it's playing to his strengths. He certainly thinks a lot about the game; he doesn't just hit it as hard as he can or bowl it as fast as possible. He's got a very good cricket brain. He's also a match-winner and they are gold dust.'

'I had a disastrous run in the slips for England in 2003, when I kept shelling out catches. So many seemed to be off Freddie, yet he was always the first to come over and say, "Never mind, mate." He knows what it's like at slip. That's one of the many reasons why he's a top bloke.'

audience, he became aware that he was on duty more often in public. He would still be the same Freddie Flintoff, enjoying a few beers with his old mates in Preston or Manchester, if not living quietly with Rachael out in the Cheshire sticks, but now and then he'd have a taste of how the glitterati passed the time. He was amused by it, stored the experience away for a conversational gambit, but vowed never to be swayed by the fleeting brush with fame.

One night, in the summer of 2003, Flintoff and Rachael dined at the Ivy, the fashionable eaterie in London's West End frequented by the thespians of the arts and their hard-eyed agents. It's a place with lots of air-kissing, adjectival excess and undying promises that my people will call your people first thing tomorrow morning, and let's do lunch soonest, darling. Hardly the place where you'd find Freddie Flintoff. But Chubby Chandler had fixed a table for two and he thought Rachael would enjoy it.

At the table next to them, the actor Michael Caine was dining. He had long been a Flintoff favourite, with his distinctive Elephant and Castle accent and unerring instinct on how to deliver a line at its best. Freddie sent a joshing text message to Chandler, saying, 'Thanks for the table, but Michael Caine won't leave me alone!' When Flintoff returned from the toilet, Caine stopped him for a word.

'He told me he liked the way I played cricket, and although I resisted the temptation to say I loved you in *The Italian Job*, I was chuffed. I asked him if he'd like to come to Lord's on Saturday, that I'd get him tickets for lunch and tea, and he said, "No thanks, mate – I only watch cricket on the telly, that's the best way." I thought that was brilliant, Michael Caine talking to me!'

At the start of the year, Flintoff had been worried that he might not make the World Cup. At the end of it, he had established a reputation for himself as a match-winner in international cricket: he was England's Man of the Series in the Tests against South Africa, having played a decisive part in the remarkable victory at The Oval; then in one-day matches, he won five Man of the Match awards out of six; he passed Ian Botham's England record of sixes in one-dayers, in half the innings that the great all-rounder needed; and he was named one of *Wisden*'s Five Cricketers of the Year when the Almanack took its decision for the 2004 edition. He was now the established all-rounder for England and confidence oozed out of him. The hard work under Dave Roberts' exacting command around the hills of Bolton had paid off.

He had managed to make the World Cup with hardly any time to spare, playing in one game against Australia in Melbourne to prove his fitness. Before the England team could buckle down to playing cricket in the World Cup, they were thrown off course by the ongoing wrangle over Zimbabwe. For months it had dragged on and, as the tournament drew nearer and nearer, the England players were locked in complicated meetings where they had to take on board matters that ought to have been sorted out much earlier. Basically, they had to decide whether to go to Zimbabwe to play one World Cup match in Harare against the host country. Should they stay away in protest against the repressive regime of Robert Mugabe, or through safety concerns, or just go there and play, because politics shouldn't impinge on sporting matters?

The issue may have appeared simple to older, more sophisticated people, but it was asking a lot of young men, wrapped up in their own sporting careers, to unravel the complexities at short notice. They were damned if they did and damned if they didn't. In the end, the unanimous decision was not to go, for safety and security reasons, with the loss of four points because England had been deemed to have forfeited the match. Flintoff resents that the players were put on the spot.

'The England players weren't paid to make such decisions, our job was to play cricket. Why was the decision suddenly thrown into our laps? Why couldn't the politicians and the game's ruling bodies get together earlier? The political wheeler-dealing left me very confused and I felt very sorry for someone like Jimmy Anderson, who'd been on board for only a few weeks and, at the age of 21, was expected to make a crucial decision. All those meetings on the eve of the World Cup were a major strain, especially on our captain Nasser Hussain. In the end, I went with the decision not to go for safety and security reasons. We owed it to our families to take the death threats seriously. But we can't use the loss of those four points as an excuse for going out of the World Cup early because those long meetings did help team spirit. When the tournament eventually started, we had become a very close unit.'

Elation at a few wickets –
Sachin Tendulkar and
Shoaib Malik (right).

It was more relevant than the Harare forfeit that England played poorly to lose to India in Durban and shouldn't have lost by two wickets to Australia in Port Elizabeth. That defeat by Australia effectively eliminated England and it was an object lesson in how to win tight games when more or less out of it. When Andy Bichel joined Michael Bevan, there was only Glenn McGrath left to lend his negligible batting to Australia's attempt to chisel out another 80 runs on a slow, low pitch. Nine times out of ten you would back the bowling side. But this was Australia and Flintoff – having played little against them in his career – could see at first hand the qualities that make them world champions.

'We were shattered to lose from that situation, but sometimes you've got to take your hat off to the opposition and this was one of those occasions. They batted fantastically well. Bevan is a brilliant finisher and he did what he does for a pastime, but Bichel has always been a handy batsman. He's scored first-class hundreds for Queensland and one for Worcestershire in a one-day game, so that's a hell of a player to come in at number ten.'

Yet Flintoff had a good World Cup, justifying his place after the fitness worries.

He'd improved as a one-day bowler and ended up as the most economical in the tournament, going for less than three an over. He was indebted to Steve Harmison for a technical tip that enabled him to maintain pace without sacrificing accuracy. Harmison wasn't featuring in the World Cup games, although part of the squad, and he'd noticed that Flintoff was fretting a little early on over his bowling.

Harmison recalls: 'He came to me and asked for some help. There were one or two things that he wasn't doing right and I just tried to simplify things. He just needed to run up and bowl naturally, something that I've had to work on myself. I just tried to get a few demons out of his mind, get him to snap his wrist more at the release of the ball. It worked and Freddie bowled really well in the World Cup.'

He batted well against India, getting a half-century in a losing cause. There was no pressure on him because wickets were falling at the other end on a regular basis, but again he showed that he was learning how to bat with the lower order. A cameo of 26 against Pakistan at Newlands hinted at his capabilities, but he was dismissed carelessly.

'The night before, at our team meeting, I was asked how we should play Pakistan's off-spinner, Saqlain Mushtaq. I found that quite flattering that my views should be asked for, especially as many outside the England camp thought I hadn't a clue how to play spinners. But I did have a good record against Saqlain whenever Surrey played Lancashire, so I was happy to pass on whatever I knew. Come the match and I'm stumped off Saqlain's bowling! Just as well we won the game, but it kept the lads going for a day or two.'

But the biggest practical lesson for Flintoff came in that Australia match. He'd

Enjoying the dismissal of
Shaun Pollock in the 2003
NatWest series against
South Africa.

Vaughan out, Flintoff in, Dambulla one-day international, 2003. And there were a lot of batsmen passing each other that day, as Sri Lanka bowled us out for 88.

Getting the hurry-up from Australia's Brett Lee in the World Cup match in Port Elizabeth, 2003. Lee is quick, I promise you!

come in at 87 for 5, aware that he must play watchfully for a time, trying to rebuild the innings. On such a slow surface, anything over a total of 200 would give England a chance – 225 would be a bonus. He'd got to 45 off 80 deliveries, extremely patient by his standards, and at 177 for 5 calmer waters lay ahead for England. If the tail played around Flintoff, that score of 225 was well within the compass.

'I'd just hit Andrew Symonds for six over mid-wicket and then, in the 44th over, decided it was time to step it up. Andy Bichel came on and I tried to smack him over mid-wicket but I got my front foot in the way and it just dollied straight up in the air.

'I'd gone big too soon. I should have carried on, pushing the ball around

Batting in a one-day international in Colombo in 2003.

I had some luck against Jacques Kallis in both the Test and one-day series against South Africa in 2003. After I top-edged him to the third man boundary, he said 'You just want to hit every ball for four, don't you?' I think Kallis didn't rate me all that highly, because he was always giving me some verbals. I kept out of his way when he batted – he's too good. Send for Harmison!

for another three overs or so, then tried the big shots from the 48th over. When you haven't lost too many wickets, you can go big with ten overs left, but you should be waiting for the last three overs when there aren't many wickets in hand. That mistake of mine could have cost us another 30 runs.' England ended up with 204 for 8 and fell agonisingly short. But this was one game that they ought to have won against Australia, to end a losing sequence in one-day games that stretched back to January 1999. And Flintoff takes his share of the blame for that Port Elizabeth defeat.

'Michael Bevan's batting gave me an insight into just how you should bat in the closing overs. Watching him work the ball around, without any fuss, was an object lesson in pacing a run chase. In our innings, I'd fallen short of what was needed towards the end of an innings. We quietly fancied ourselves to make the Super Sixes, despite losing four points over Zimbabwe, and if we'd beaten the Aussies that day, we'd have been there. Anything can happen after that.'

If Flintoff needed any further amplification about how to bat in the latter stages, it came in a conversation during the World Cup with two of his heroes. He'd bumped into Wasim Akram in a hotel bar and fell into genial banter with his old Lancashire team-mate, who had never stinted in his

public support for Flintoff when he first came into the England team and encountered some caustic criticism. Wasim introduced him to Sir Viv Richards, which just about made Flintoff's tournament, never mind his day.

'I didn't expect Viv to be bothered about giving me the time of day and, to be honest, I was a bit tongue-tied in the presence of such an awesome cricketer. There's still an aura about the man, even when he walks into a room. Anyway, he was fantastic to me, called me "Fred", and said he liked my approach to the game. I was thrilled he knew so much about me and then he offered me advice about how to bat at the end of a limited-overs match. He said, "You've got to get in, Fred, and no matter how many balls you've got left at the death, you'll get them. But you must stay in, to establish yourself first. No early risks." When Viv talks about batting, then you hang on his every word.'

So Flintoff returned to England in March, bent on putting more thought into his batting, with Richards' words fresh in his mind. He decided to enlist the specialist talents of the Lancashire coach, Mike Watkinson. Known to everyone as 'Winker' Watkinson, he had been a fine all-rounder for Lancashire, good enough to play for England in the mid-nineties and totally up to speed with the modern game, having just retired. He'd rated Flintoff as a player since he first came onto the Lancashire staff, had been at the other end when Flintoff scored his maiden first-class century and was trusted by him. Flintoff wanted an extra dimension to the batting coaching he was getting, and Watkinson's ability to bowl both off-spin and seamers was a great advantage. He'd always valued Watkinson's ability to talk sense about cricket and, like Dave Roberts in fitness terms, could rely on the plain, unvarnished truth from him. He needed that if he was to progress as an international batsman.

When working one-to-one in March and April of 2003, Watkinson would simulate match conditions and challenge his pupil. He would select a proper, shiny ball, so that it would swing when he bowled at Flintoff. Then he'd deliver it from around 17 yards, rather than the accustomed 22, so that the batsman

MIKE WATKINSON
Lancashire coach and England assistant coach

'In international cricket, Freddie seems to play well once he reaches 30, so it then becomes second nature to him. Working with him off 17 yards before the 2003 season appeared to reduce his vulnerability at the start of his innings. That support structure is important to Freddie, because it takes away uncertainty over how he should be preparing himself. He doesn't need wishy-washy advice, he's the sort who needs to be told what to do.

'When we were in Sri Lanka, he murdered the other spinners, apart from Murali. The ball was flying back over their heads every five minutes. I've seen him do the same for Lancashire. He's not the only one to have struggled against Murali.'

would need to sharpen up his reactions. Flintoff's fast hands and sharp reactions had often got him out of trouble when playing too early or away from his body. He needed to play closer to the ball.

'Winker is still a fierce competitor and he tried to get me out every ball. He'd "ooh" and "ah", appeal for anything close and just get in my face, trying to ruffle me. With his all-round bowling skills, he certainly made me feel uncomfortable off 17 yards. He thought I was reaching too far out for the ball from 22 yards and this way would make me play tighter around off-stump, to make sure I didn't lose the shape of my shots. Winker said my strokes had to come from a more compact area, rather than play flamboyantly in the air when slightly off-balance. That five yards difference made me stop playing ahead of myself, reducing the risk of pushing firmly at the ball, one of my weaknesses in the past.'

Several of the other Lancashire batsmen tapped into this exercise as well during pre-season. They'd say, 'Are you ready for a masterclass, Winker?' and

disappear with him and a box of balls. Perhaps that's one of the reasons why Lancashire's batsmen scored so many runs in the 2003 season. It certainly worked for Flintoff. Throughout that summer, he'd seek out Watkinson before the start of play or at the close and go through the routine, and they carried it on in Sri Lanka when Watkinson came out as England's assistant coach. With England during the 2003 season, Phil Neale would play Watkinson's role. That grooving of technique and reactions undoubtedly played a part in Flintoff's consistent batting during that golden summer. He was also very fit and confident about his own game. The pieces were starting to fit snugly.

He began the season for Lancashire in majestic form and it simply carried on all season. A hundred against Middlesex on a flat wicket, 97 against Nottinghamshire and 154 at Canterbury against Kent were an excellent platform for the summer ahead. The hundred against Kent was particularly gratifying because Lancashire were 52 for 5 on the first morning and he then blitzed 154 off 158 balls, including eight sixes. Mark Ealham, an old England team-mate, had taken four of the first five wickets, troubling everyone with his late swing.

The Lancashire coach, Mike Watkinson has had a big influence on my batting since I came back from the 2003 World Cup. He stretches me, and as I know from the days when he was a team-mate, he talks a lot of common sense.

Flintoff has often struggled against such a canny bowler, but not this time.

'I pinged my first ball straight back over Ealy's head and I thought, "That felt all right." It was a checked drive and it felt as sweet as a nut. I felt it might just be my day.'

In between overs, Flintoff chatted away to that genial umpire, John Holder. Flintoff felt very relaxed at the crease and was pleased to hear Holder say that he now looked a much better cricketer than a year ago; that he seemed to have matured at last. He agreed, but anti-climax was close at hand.

'The very next over, I tried to knock a ball from outside off-stump into Canterbury city centre. I missed it completely, it was my only false shot, but a horrible one. Yet I was so relaxed that I burst out laughing as the ball went through to the keeper. I turned round to look at John Holder, standing at square leg and he was on the floor, laughing his head off!'

Flintoff entertained many more than John Holder in the summer of 2003. He gladdened the hearts of those who value personality in sport and relish seeing a top player relax and just go with the flow of inspiration. In the South African Test series, he not only averaged over 50 and took ten good wickets – when with luck it would have been nearer 20 – but he hit 14 sixes. That's twice as many as Ian Botham plundered during his 'annus mirabilis' against the Australians in 1981, the summer of dramatic derring-do from the great all-rounder. Flintoff was now starting to shape Test matches to his own will by sheer force of personality and skill. Television punters delayed putting the kettle on when Flintoff was batting, while the fans at the ground let the queue for beers carry on without them. Flintoff was at the crease and very few rushed to the bar. The bowlers often complained about the ball getting out of shape when Flintoff was out there, swatting them.

The confidence Flintoff now felt about his game allowed him to express himself out in the middle, to trust his instincts when batting. He got into better positions at the crease, looked tighter in defence, leaving balls more often outside the off-stump.

'When I'm batting well, I give off the impression that I haven't got a care in the world, and I saunter around. I have to work at controlling the adrenalin rush because I know that often gets me out. It's almost impossible trying not to let the tension show and that's when I shout at myself, or do those silly dances to get my feet moving.

The moment when I broke my bat, smashing a ball from Makhaya Ntini in the Lord's Test against South Africa in 2003.

'It's almost as if I feel I have to do something. Concentration is a problem for me. I'm not one of those who can get "in the zone", as they say, but now I know I've got those windows where I have to switch on. I'm good at switching off – it's getting back into it that's my difficulty. When the fast bowler has delivered the ball, I switch off right away and only focus again

One of my sixes at The Oval, when I scored 95 against South Africa in 2003. This one felt sweet as a nut!

when he's approaching the umpire. I find it's hard to flick that switch back on at just the right time, but presumably that comes with experience. Mike Atherton was fantastic at that.'

Flintoff had looked in very good order in the first Test at Edgbaston against the South Africans, only to be torpedoed for 40 by one that kept horribly low and trapped him lbw. But in the next Test, at Lord's, he smashed his second Test hundred – 142 off 146 balls, with five sixes and 18 fours. That day, his power

was not only reminiscent of Botham at his most brutal, but it was hard to recall, 20 years on, the ball being hit harder by the great man. Flintoff even broke one of his bats and the packed crowd enjoyed the sight of him waving the splintered blade like a giant toothpick, waiting for a replacement from the England dressing-room.

For a couple of hours on that sunny afternoon, Flintoff gave great entertainment, taking 20 off one over from Shaun Pollock with some blistering shots. By then, Flintoff was just enjoying himself because the game was lost and he's never been one for individual aggrandisement. Steve Harmison had come in at number ten, determined to usher Flintoff to his hundred. But Flintoff was by now starting to nominate his shots before the bowler delivered the ball. Harmison chided him: 'Come on Freddie! A hundred's a hundred – get your name on that board in the dressing-room!' When he reached the landmark, Flintoff's low-key, sheepish acknowledgement of the raucous ovation for a marvellously entertaining innings spoke volumes. It wasn't going to be a landmark in his career.

'My first Test hundred was much more relevant, because that helped us win the match. At Lord's, it had no great relevance at that stage to the match. We were about to lose by an innings after they'd hammered us for almost 700. The crowd loved it and I'm glad that my couple of hours in the sun stopped them going home too early, but the fact is that we lost that Test heavily, so there was nothing to celebrate about.'

Fielding in the deep in front of my home crowd at Old Trafford.

Still the memory of that Pollock over – lifting him over long-off for six, then creaming him through extra cover for two classy boundaries, all in the same over – remained fresh in the minds of all cricket lovers after Lord's, irrespective of the result. Genuine fans of the game, no matter how patriotic, can live with defeat so long as they have consolations and they see cricket played with panache and character. Shaun Pollock has rarely been treated with such cavalier disdain in his distinguished Test career and Flintoff's assault, from an impressive technical base, will be cherished long after the main protagonists have forgotten that compelling duel in the sun.

Just over a month later, Flintoff was granted his wish – an innings by him that was satisfying from a personal point of view which also contributed to victory. And what a victory! The nine-wicket win came at the end of an epic encounter, one of the best Test matches in recent years in England. It squared the series at 2-2, while the sentimentalists enjoyed the sight of Alec Stewart being chaired around his beloved Oval at the end to signify his last game of Test cricket. One of those lending a brawny shoulder to carry Stewart was Andrew Flintoff – the quintessential old pro being feted by a young man who had finally come of age as an influential Test cricketer, five years after being given his first Test cap by Stewart.

Batting with Steve Harmison in The Oval Test of 2003 against South Africa, when Harmy kept me concentrating hard, telling me I could get a hundred. He was wrong – I got 95 – but our stand of 99 gave us the impetus to win the game.

Yet at the end of that first day at The Oval, England appeared in disarray. South Africa may have lost a wicket to the final ball of the day, but at 362 for 4, the foundations for a massive score had been confidently laid. Jacques Kallis, the world's best all-rounder was still there, 32 not out, intent on signing off an interrupted summer with a big score. The South Africans were at full strength for the first time in the series they had triumphed impressively at Leeds in the previous Test to go 2-1 up in the series, and with two fine days forecast, followed by three rainy ones, how could South Africa lose from here? England had been insipid in the field on that first day as Herschelle Gibbs plundered a brilliant hundred and the bookmakers gave their own dismissive verdict on England's chances on that Thursday night: 40-1 against an England victory. From what we'd seen on that opening day, it was hard to demur.

But they came back hard at South Africa on the second morning, vigorously making things happen, showing spirit in the field. South Africa were all out for

I still don't get enough Test wickets yet to take any of them for granted. This one – getting Shaun Pollock at Trent Bridge – was important because it helped seal our victory in the 2003 series.

RIGHT AND BELOW Enjoying myself during my hundred in the Lord's Test against South Africa in 2003. By this stage of my innings, with an innings defeat just round the corner, I was pre-selecting my shots. Perhaps that's why they were going a long way.

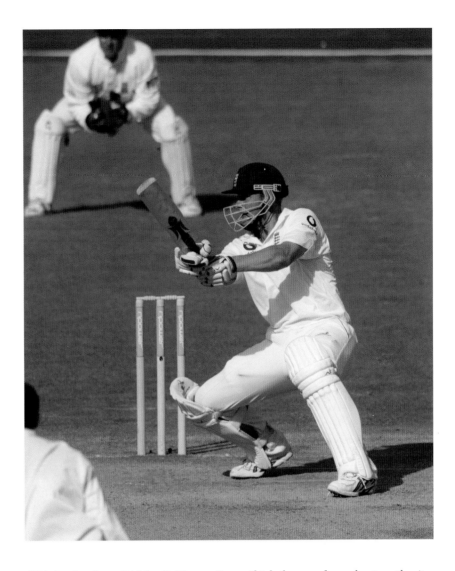

484, having been 345 for 2. Marcus Trescothick then made a robust, authoritative double hundred, while Graham Thorpe, restored after 14 months in the wilderness only because Nasser Hussain was injured, crafted a serene, pragmatic century. But with a hurricane expected to deposit some peripheral moisture in the vicinity of The Oval over the next two days, no one expected an England victory at the close on the third day, with the lead just 18 and three wickets left.

But one of those wickets was Andrew Flintoff's. On that Saturday night, he had batted with uncommon restraint, finishing ten not out. Some were surprised that he hadn't opted to flog some tired bowling near the end of a long day, but he was mindful of the words of his coach before going in to bat. Duncan Fletcher had forecast that a total of around 600, giving a lead of about 120, would put the South Africans under pressure. Flintoff, by now used to batting with the tail in both forms of international cricket, knew his role. He'd play for the morrow and hope to choose his moment correctly when he moved onto the attack.

The juices flowing at The Oval, as one of my sixes disappears against the South Africans when I made 95.

Bowling at Lord's in the second Test against South Africa in 2003.

Next day – fine and bright, with no sign of the hurricane – Martin Bicknell was out immediately. This was a blow because Bicknell is an experienced, capable batsman, which is more than can be said for Flintoff's next partner, Steve Harmison. The front foot thrust with an angled bat, allied to a measure of bloody-mindedness, is more or less the sum total of what Harmison had to offer as an England batsman at that stage, but he knew what was needed. They added 99 and Harmison's part in that was just three. Straight away, he was cajoling his great friend – 'I won't get out, Freddie' – and he was as good as his word.

He remembers: 'I could see that Freddie was thinking of smashing every ball when I first came in, so my job was to calm him down. I said if he could pick and choose more carefully, he'd help us win the Test. I told him to get to his fifty, then got him thinking about anything other than the cricket in between overs. We'd speak about someone we saw in the crowd or what was going in one of the stands, just having a laugh to ease the tension. If Freddie's smiling, he plays better.'

After such a careful reconnaissance, Flintoff slipped through the gears. Two massive sixes, off Makhaya Ntini's far from negligible pace, disappeared into the hospitality boxes at the Pavilion End, a long carry for those who know The Oval. They were beautifully timed, played inside out, with Flintoff moving away to legside, yet hitting through the line so sweetly, eyes firmly fixed on the ball. The crowd babbled in excitement as the bowlers were in disarray and, for the first time in the series, the South Africans lost their discipline in the field. Their mature young captain, Graeme Smith, at last looked vulnerable – as you do when an opponent's brilliance changes the shape of a Test in the blink of an eye.

Flintoff made the last 85 of his runs off just 72 balls. Another century was there for the taking. The bowlers contrived to avoid their captain's eyes as he kept shuffling them around, trying desperately for some control. Harmison told his mate he'd get him to his hundred.

'I think Harmy was more worried about that than me – that I was going to get carried away. The noise from the crowd was fantastic. I don't know how cricketers can say they can block out the sound. I can hear what just one person is saying at times, never mind 20,000 of them at The Oval when I'm whacking the ball around. So my adrenalin fed off the excitement generated by those excited, noisy supporters. I loved the occasion, the way the South Africans wilted. We could sense the game moving towards us in the space of no time at all.'

Eventually, he tried one exotic shot too many. Aiming to reach his hundred in the grand manner by lifting Paul Adams over mid-wicket, Flintoff was bowled. He was roared back up the pavilion steps and the disarray shown by the South Africans, in contrast to the English ebullience, assuaged any sense of disappointment at falling short of what would have been a wonderful century.

'I'll take a score of 95 every time I walk to the crease in a Test match. I was a bit surprised, though, by a comment from one of the umpires later in the day when we were fielding. Venkat said to me, "You don't like getting hundreds, do you?" I thought that a bit harsh – I was only five runs short. Anyway, I've always seen it as a team game and, in going for the quick runs on that Sunday morning, I felt I was doing the right thing to give us time to bowl them out. We'd frustrated them and when they came out to bat, they were out of sorts, vulnerable to the pressure we exerted.'

With the lead a precious 120, England bowled far better than on that first day, with Harmison – confidence boosted by his batting – at last looking the part of an England bowler. He took 4 for 33 in 19 hostile overs, as South Africa folded to 229 all out. England raced home, scoring the 110 needed at five an over. It had been an astonishing comeback, with enough sub-plots to keep any scribe happy. But for two England players it was a highly significant Test match. Harmison built on the confidence he displayed when bowling in the second innings, proceeding to decimate Bangladesh a few months later in the first Test, then laying the West Indies to waste, bowling especially well against Brian Lara. Those 24 hours at The Oval, when Harmison impressed with bat and ball, could prove a watershed in the career of a cricketer who thrives on self-confidence.

Then there was Andrew Flintoff. He was a hero at last to the English sporting

A sight I got used to during the 2003 Test series against South Africa – Graeme Smith clipping me away for a legside four.

public, not just for the way he was playing, but for the consistency he showed. No longer the frustrating, flashing meteor, he had arrived. It had been a long and at times painful journey, with some of the detours of his own making.

'That 95 was much more valuable than the hundred at Lord's. It demonstrated that I could play maturely and patiently while waiting for the time to cut loose. I was so chuffed that I ended the Test series and the summer on a high. Being named England's Man of the Series was an extra thrill because it meant I'd been consistent. I felt I belonged in the England team at long last. My slow progress had been partly my own fault, with some bad luck over injuries thrown in, but the relaxed style of our new captain was good for me.

Smith is finally out in the 2003 series, after hitting two unbeaten double hundreds. I got him to hit his wicket at Trent Bridge. He couldn't believe it. They all count!

'Michael Vaughan made me feel liberated under his captaincy. He just told me to have a go if I think I can clear the boundary. He said he didn't want to see me plodding along, but to play the way that suited my style, and to be seen with a smile on my face. With Vaughany's encouragement, I finally felt as if I belonged on the big stage. The doubts had been pushed into the background.'

For his part, Vaughan has thought long and hard about the best way to handle Flintoff: 'In the last year, I've noticed he's been a lot more focused when we're at work. Perhaps in the past, he's let other things bother him but he's quieter now and just gets on with it. He practises hard, and with a purpose. These days, Freddie seems to have his head stuck in a book a lot of the time, even though he can be loud at certain times – especially when we've won. Everyone thinks Freddie's big, bold and macho but underneath he's quite an insecure lad. He hasn't forgotten the bad times or all those injuries. He's a loveable big bear really, who has to be treated in the right manner. People have got to realise he's only human, even though there's a lot of euphoria built up around him these days. We've got to manage him properly and help him keep his focus.'

Flintoff's value to England was demonstrated when he was ordered to rest at home rather than travel to Bangladesh a few weeks later for two Test matches. He had felt a slight tweak in the groin during The Oval Test, and after bowling more overs than any other English player in the series, it was felt that the challenge of

Sri Lanka and the West Indies a few months later was more pressing. The previous year, Flintoff's welfare didn't appear to be of primary concern as his slow recovery from his hernia operation was greeted sceptically in some quarters of Team England. But the long-overdue appointment of a Chief Medical Officer by the ECB had introduced a more rational approach to serious injuries, with Dr Peter Gregory taking over the responsibility that shouldn't rest with the overworked England physiotherapist on tour. Hopefully, under Dr Gregory's authority, Flintoff will prove to be the last England player to be put through such an erratic mangle.

When Flintoff finally got out to Bangladesh, for the one-day internationals, he dominated the series. He won the Man of the Match for all three games, as they followed a familiar pattern. Bangladesh would make a low score and Flintoff would come in, scatter sixes all over the ground and win the match with overs to spare.

In the three games, Flintoff made 177 runs off just 138 balls, without being

My turn to bat in the nets in Sri Lanka, 2003.

A great day for all England sports supporters, as England win the rugby World Cup to beat Australia. I'm in a bar in Colombo, Sri Lanka savouring the moment with (far left) Graham Thorpe, (back row left) Paul Collingwood,(left) Matthew Hoggard and (back row right) James Kirtley.

dismissed. Of those runs, 132 came in boundaries, including ten sixes. In that period, he passed Ian Botham's record of sixes for England in one-day internationals. Botham hit 44 in his 106 one-day innings, while Flintoff passed him in just 56. His strike-rate per hundred balls was also far superior to that of Botham – 88.5 to 78.81. Flintoff scored 65 per cent of England's runs in that Bangladesh series, a phenomenal mastery of the opposition by one man. Agreed, it was men against boys, given the poverty of the opposition, but England have made hard work of such situations before on many occasions. Not this time, thanks to Flintoff's dominance.

'I enjoyed the whole experience of Bangladedsh, apart from the heat and humidity. The hotels were fine, the food good and the players managed to spend a lot of time together because there was very little to do outside the hotel. I think that close-knit atmosphere we created out there served us well when we got to the West Indies. We'd talked a lot about strategies and how to

Next man in, Colombo 2003. Not an enjoyable time – it could be hours, or the next minute.

No offence, Mr Vaughan, sir – but it's been a long day, we've lost a one-dayer in Sri Lanka, the awards ceremony is taking ages to start and I'd like to be in my hotel room now, please!

deal with the inevitable setbacks on the field, so we were a tough, integrated unit when we arrived in the Caribbean.'

Flintoff and the rest of the England squad knew that Sri Lanka would provide a far sterner test than Bangladesh before they returned home for Christmas, and so it proved. A couple of desperate rearguard actions kept them in the series until the final Test at Colombo, but then England folded in the draining heat and humidity to lose by an innings. Flintoff managed to redeem himself against the spinners in that match by scoring 107 in the two innings. He needed to restore some credibility on the sub-continent after his personal horrors in India two years earlier. Coping with the wiles of Muttiah Muralitharan was an even greater challenge than Anil Kumble. Flintoff and Murali are very fond of each other, dating back to the Sri Lankan's time with Lancashire when Flintoff was characteristically hospitable to him, ensuring homesickness was at least kept at bay as he diddled out stacks of baffled county batsmen. But in a Test series, Murali's loyalties lay emphatically with his country, rather than his old team-mate. He'd smile and share a joke with Flintoff at the non-striker's end, but not when bowling at him.

'Murali's a genius, and there's no disgrace in getting out to him. Nobody knows which way the ball's going to turn and he's made fools of better

MUTTIAH MURALITHARAN

Lancashire team-mate and Sri Lankan spinner

'Freddie played very well against me in the Colombo Test.
He played patiently, defended well and knocked the ball around
against the other spinners. He also bowled very well in the heat.
Michael Vaughan could just throw him the ball and he'd keep
coming at you, at almost 90 miles an hour – a very brave
cricketer. And a lovely man, my best friend in English cricket.
He always keeps in touch and when I first came to Lancashire,
he took me around to show me all the sights.'

batsmen than me. When he played with us at Lancashire I watched him very closely, trying to work him out in the nets, but still he's too good for me. In this series, he got me out lbw twice and he said, "Freddie, why do you play back to me?" All I could offer was, "It's all right for you – you should try batting against your bowling!"'

Flintoff thought long and hard about how to combat Muralitharan. For once in his career, he decided to block a bowler, to frustrate him.

'At Colombo, I just kicked him away, keeping the bat out of the way as often as possible, while watching out for the extra bounce that might take my gloves. Then I'd climb into the other spinners, who didn't faze me.'

He smashed four sixes in his 77 in the first innings, with the leg-spinner Upul Chandana conceding three of them. Chaminda Vaas, that fine swing bowler, was deposited over mid-wicket for another nonchalant six, then a crunching straight drive off Vaas almost took off the head of umpire Alim Dar, who opted for an undignified dive to the ground for safety. A total of 64 in boundaries

Reflecting on a heavy one-day defeat by Sri Lanka in 2003. Sometimes a cold beer and some solitude are necessary.

I'm almost the hat-trick dismissal for Muttiah Muralitharan in the Colombo Test of 2003, as I glove my first ball just past Hashan Tillekeratne. I hung around for ages after that for 30, but at least Murali didn't get me!

suggests a typical Flintoff ratio for an innings of 77, but he was a deal more circumspect second time around, not least because Murali was at him throughout. His 30 took 75 balls, but six boundaries illuminated the comparatively dour canvas. At least, though, he showed he was learning how to bat in alien conditions against the spinners.

So the year ended with Andrew Flintoff established as an integral part of the England team. He was now resisting the urge to plonk most balls out of the ground. The 'leave alone' shot looked almost a natural course of action to him as Mike Watkinson's tutelage had become inculcated. It would have been agreeable to Flintoff if more catches had been taken off his bowling, but he

Coping somehow with the humidity of Bangladesh in 2003. I struggle in the heat and humidity of the sub-continent, the perspiration just pours out of me as soon as I get out of the air-conditioning.

Running the gauntlet of the traders in Dhaka, 2003. Don't think this bloke had my size!

It's not just in Manchester where cricketers have to deal with the rain. But it's warm rain – Sri Lanka 2003.

One of those days at the office where it can get very frustrating – during the Kandy Test against Sri Lanka in 2003. I bowled 39 overs in the game and didn't have a great deal of luck.

Breaking free of the shackles in the third Test in Colombo, when I scored 77. I blocked Muttiah Muralitharan at the other end and climbed into the other bowlers, who weren't so threatening.

wouldn't be throwing his rattle out of the pram over that. He was just grateful to be fit and confident that he'd be able to face all the physical demands of the modern international cricketer. Within a few months he had become the heartbeat of the national side and its most popular player because of his gusto and spirit. Next stop, the Caribbean – a place where charismatic cricketers are hugely appreciated.

MICHAEL VAUGHAN

England captain

'I think he deals with failures a bit better than he used to. We saw that in Sri Lanka after he'd had two bad Tests with the bat. Two years earlier he probably wouldn't have gone out and scored those runs at Colombo because he would have convinced himself that he wasn't going to get any. But he worked hard on his game leading up to the Colombo Test and that proved to me that he's mentally stronger now.'

With my fiancée, Rachael Wools. She has been terrific for me, helping me focus on my cricket at the right times, and then switch off, to enjoy a life away from it all.

There's a time and place. It's just knowing when and where to relax and enjoy a pint.

OVERLEAF Training near my home in Cheshire before the 2004 tour to West Indies.

CHAPTER 6

Staying at the Top

ike the England team as a whole, Andrew Flintoff had a marvellous tour of the Caribbean. Three-nil winners in the Test series, giving them victory there for the first time since 1968, Flintoff averaged 50 with the bat, 27 with the ball and took some terrific catches with aplomb at slip. He made a patient century to help save the Antigua Test, took five wickets in a Test innings for the first time and looked as if he'd hold his place as the all-rounder in any side in the world. Yet the key to that impressive series of performances had come a fortnight before the tour started, at Loughborough University.

Our aggression in the field was a feature of our success in the Caribbean. We were at the West Indies all the time.

The England squad assembled at the Academy headquarters in Lough-borough for a few days before departure for a final round of meetings, nets and fitness tests. With such a competitive bunch, the challenge was on to find out which player had the best all-round fitness record. The disciplines involved the dreaded 'bleep' tests, which measure the cardio-vascular levels, then a stint on the rowing machine, some uphill running, sit-ups, press-ups, step-ups with weights and then without them – all against the clock. The record time had been set by Simon Jones 15 months earlier, just before he left for his ill-fated tour of Australia. Jones is a naturally gifted athlete, which had helped aid his recovery after his horrendous knee injury in the Brisbane Test. This time, Jones' record was shattered by Andrew Flintoff.

Even Duncan Fletcher was impressed and said 'well done' to Flintoff. Nobody

MICHAEL VAUGHAN
England captain

'Freddie likes being a father figure to the younger players.

He realises he made mistakes when young and realises probably

more than anyone else what are the pitfalls when you come into

the team. Your earning potential changes and you can let it affect

you. He's the first to admit that he may have let it affect him.

Hopefully, the youngsters will end up like he is now.'

in the England camp had expected Flintoff to come out ahead of everyone else – including the young zealots attending the Academy – but not for the first time in his career, they'd misjudged Flintoff. His sheer physical strength had never been in doubt, more his dedication to get as fit as possible. But Dave Roberts' words kept clanging around in his brain and now the player wanted to prove much to himself. It was a favourable portent for Flintoff's tour. And in second place was Steve Harmison. He breezed through the tests, much to his great friend's delight. And Harmison didn't have a bad tour of the Caribbean, either.

Harmison's 23 wickets in the four Tests gave him the Man of the Series award. He simply blew the West Indies batsmen away in the first two Tests, but what impressed everyone was the way he kept pounding in at Antigua against Brian Lara after he had passed the 300 mark. Harmison didn't know when he was beaten. After he'd taken 7 for 12 in the first Test in Jamaica, with West Indies bowled out for just 47, Harmison sat in the dressing-room in a daze. Flintoff said to him, 'You just don't know what you've done, do you?' Flintoff had a greater awareness of what people would be saying back home after such an astonishing victory by ten wickets after losing the toss.

In the West Indies with Troy Cooley, our excellent bowling coach, who has done so much for England's five fast bowlers on the tour – from left, myself, Steve Harmison, Simon Jones, Matthew Hoggard and James Anderson.

'When you're thousands of miles from home, you can get wrapped up in yourselves and fail to realise what something like this means at home. I'd had to return early through injury from tours often enough, and got used to people putting the boot in, and Harmy had taken a lot of flak himself. So we needed to savour the moment. I didn't realise we'd have three of those in a row!'

That first victory was sufficiently significant for Flintoff to break his self-imposed alcohol ban. He hadn't touched a drop since arriving in the Caribbean, but he was so delighted for his close friend that a few tots of rum were imbibed on the night of 14 March. He could also reflect on his own satisfactory performance, backing up the other fast bowlers with some hostile, accurate work, batting well for his 46 at a run a ball, and taking three slip catches with the minimum of fuss. Two of them snared Brian Lara to give him just seven runs in the match, a vital statistic given Lara's continuing pre-eminence as a Test batsman and his outstanding record against England.

'Sabina Park was good for slip catching because the ball was bouncing, had pace and good carry, so I could see the nicks all the way. But when someone like Lara is at the crease, you concentrate even more than normal because you don't want to put down a player like him. That started me off on a purple patch in the slips for the rest of the series, which was fantastic. But I'll never forget that I've shelled out a few in there in my time.'

His batting in that first Test was tantalisingly impressive, but ended annoyingly, just as he was looking solid. Batting at number six, he'd come in at 194 for 4, in reply to the West Indies' 311, with the match evenly poised. A couple of hours of Flintoff at his best and the pendulum would have swung England's way. He had played with ease to reach 46 off 50 balls, creaming five classy bound-aries, when the occasional, undemanding legspin of Ramnaresh Sarwan was introduced into the attack. Flintoff had been moving his feet well, get-ting into the right positions, timing the ball beauti-fully. Given the tense state of the Test, he still looked as if he was cruising through a practice match. But Sarwan had him caught at mid-wicket as he'd aimed for a straight drive over long-on. It looked a soft dismissal and Flintoff was annoyed at himself.

'I'd gone out there with a game plan. Keep the scoreboard ticking over, play the shots if the ball demands it, don't get stuck. I felt very confident. When Sarwan came on, I knew the second new ball was due, and judging by the influence it had so far in the Test, that was going to be a crucial time, when perhaps the run-scoring opportunities would be reduced. I wanted to be there for the new ball, but that shot was on. It wasn't a case of being disrespectful to the bowler, more that it's a shot I play well. But I didn't get into the best position and just cuffed it to mid-wicket when it was supposed to go straight back over his head. And normally that's a safe shot for me when the ball isn't

Getting my reactions sharpened up in the indoor nets at Old Trafford, just before leaving for the West Indies, early in 2004.

turning. I get out to that stroke now and then, but often hit sixes with it. You can't have it both ways. If I was in the same situation again, I'd look to play it better – but I wouldn't duck out of trying that shot again.'

That mode of dismissal set the pattern for all but one of Flintoff's five innings in the Test series. In Trinidad, he was caught and bowled off a leading edge

The Jamaica Test of 2004 and I've just caught Brian Lara for the second time in the match. Always the key West Indian wicket. We didn't bank on him getting just seven runs in the two innings.

after looking very comfortable in making 23 off 24 balls. In Barbados, Flintoff batted watchfully to make 15 off 31 balls, happily playing the junior role to Graham Thorpe's magnificent century that decided the match. When Tino Best dropped one short just outside the off-stump, Flintoff got into the right position to punch one through the covers, one of his trademark strokes that has brought him stacks of runs. But he didn't quite get over it and was caught at cover. It was simply a matter of the right decision-making when playing attacking shots. You have to take Flintoff in the round, rather than berate him for getting himself out the over after lauding him for a dismissive boundary, perfectly timed and executed.

He admits his last dismissal of the series was a shocker. When he came in at Antigua on the final afternoon, the game was almost safe for England after Michael Vaughan's century and prolonged defiance by Marcus Trescothick and Mark Butcher. Sarwan came back to tease Flintoff and at 14, he succumbed again, smacking a full toss to mid-wicket. No excuses from Flintoff: 'It was a horrendous dismissal. That's an innings I'd rather forget. Maybe I'd subconsciously relaxed because we felt we were safe, but that ball should have disappeared.'

That's four of his five innings dealt with, but what do those who despaired of Flintoff for these soft dismissals make of his 102 not out in Antigua? He batted for more than six hours in an impressive display of self-denial to use up valuable time in the face of West Indies' massive 751 for 5 declared. Coming in at 98 for 4, he immediately lost the doughty Thorpe, then he had to nurse Geraint Jones – on his Test debut – and the tail through to some sort of a score. The follow-on was inevitable but what was more relevant was the time taken up in dismissing England, bolstered by Flintoff's indomitable example. His faithful ally, Steve Harmison, was there

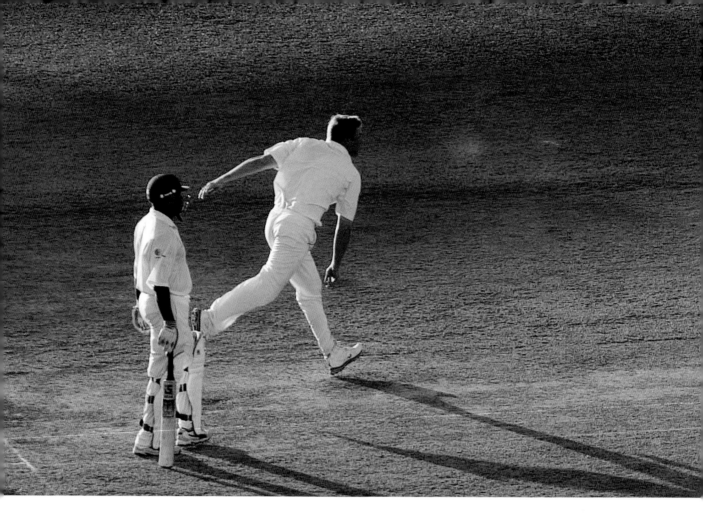

again, coaxing Flintoff to another hundred, refusing to buckle against the frustrated bowlers. Lord's, The Oval, Antigua: three important partnerships from these two in the space of nine months.

An innings of 102 off 224 balls, with just 58 of them coming in boundaries, is not a typical piece of scoring by Andrew Flintoff – but that's why this was such an impressive effort by him. He understood the exigencies of the situation and drew on his recent experiences of batting with the tail to organise the resistance. He was technically smart enough to combat some excellent reverse swing by Pedro Collins by reducing his backlift considerably to negate late movement. The red mists descended only for a time when Fidel Edwards tried to ruffle him with some hostile stares, but Flintoff proceeded to cuff him around disdainfully. A flat hooked six and a pulverising square cut in the same Edwards' over were the perfect ripostes to such posturing as he moved calmly to his third Test hundred. It was not one that shaped a victory as in Christchurch, or a jolly thrash in a losing cause as at Lord's, but this one contributed to a draw. That is never an ignoble aim by a number six batsman in a Test match.

He had a few slices of luck along the way. He was missed at slip and gully, and by Collins off his own bowling as he failed to cling onto a howitzer that whizzed straight back at him. But earlier, the England players were convinced

Near the end of play in the second Test in Trinidad, as I try for one more wicket. Ridley Jacobs looks happy enough to stay at his end.

that Lara had been caught behind off Harmison before he had scored even one of his 400 runs. These things even themselves out and not even Flintoff's harshest detractors can deny that some shocking decisions have gone against him in Tests. His equable reactions to those errors have done him credit.

'I can't honestly remember getting away with dropped catches before when batting for England – I either get fired out, get myself out or the fielder clings onto the chance – so I reckon I was due some luck. Lara should have caught me at slip. It was a difficult chance in the gully, but I don't regard that one to the bowler as a chance. I really hit it hard and was disappointed not to get a four for it. This was a big innings for me because I had a job to do after getting out to some average shots earlier in the series. I wanted us to use up enough overs so that they had to take the second new ball. That way they'd be more tired when we followed on and they might not get into us early, with one day left. It took them 99 overs to get us out and they did look tired when our openers went out for the second innings. When Vaughan and Trescothick put on such a big opening stand second time around that was decisive in getting us the draw.

'I'm glad my different attitude helped me grind out that hundred, because I know I can play like that and will have to do so more often for

JOHN CRAWLEY

Former Lancashire and England team-mate

'He bats better with people who know him well and can see if he's getting over-anxious or disrespectful of the bowling. Just keep him concentrating. I've got no worries about his ability to play the spinners, his undoing is often the dibbly-dobbly swingers at medium pace who bore him out.'

'He was unbelievable for me to captain. He could win you anything in a run chase and would just keep going with the ball, giving you control and pace. He would never say "no" at any stage of the game – a captain's dream. I think he'd enjoy captaining Lancashire when he's eventually right for the job – but not sure how he'd take to all those meetings!'

England when necessary. I'm wondering now why I didn't play like that in the first three Test matches. I played like that for Lancashire in the 2003 season, but maybe I'd forgotten just how to construct an innings. When you bat number six, you've got to be flexible in your approach.'

It was a mature innings, an authentic hundred in the context of a Test match, where occupation of the crease is a priority. It may prove a turning point for Flintoff – proof that he isn't just a crash, bang, wallop batsman, that a sharp cricket brain does lurk behind the macho façade. His Lancashire team-mates have never doubted that. Many of them recall his sturdy defiance at The Oval in 2001, when he and John Crawley batted together for 41 overs to defy Surrey and earn a draw. Saqlain Mushtaq and Ian Salisbury operated in harness throughout, but they were negated with some ease. Crawley's technical mastery of spin has long been accepted, but his younger partner, batting at number three, made an impressive 34 and never looked out of his depth.

John Crawley recalls Flintoff's obduracy that day: 'The ball was turning a lot on the final day and we had no chance of winning, so the next best thing was to deny Surrey. We were both chasing the title and we had to stick close to them. Basically, Freddie hit the ball in the middle of the bat when playing defensively. He watched the ball very closely. Saqlain was a top spinner around that time, especially in county cricket, but all Freddie had to do was concentrate hard and his good technique got him through. I'm always more interested in watching him battle it out rather than marmalise the bowlers, because battling goes against his nature. There's something freakish about the effortless way he hits sixes – you can't teach that. But when he knuckles down and plays like he did at The Oval, then in Barbados, you see his real potential as a batsman.'

At the end of the West Indies series, Geoffrey Boycott said that Flintoff was now 'a serious cricketer'. This was high praise from the apostle of percentage cricket, the advocate of getting everything you can out of yourself as a crick-

Our bowling coach, Troy Cooley has worked hard at streamlining my action. It still looks hard work, but there's not as much huffing and puffing as there used to be.

Training with England is competitive, but fun.

eter, eschewing fripperies. Boycott, chalk and cheese to Flintoff in so many ways, had been out there, working for BBC Radio and had enthused at the developing all-round skills of Flintoff. He had always admired Ian Botham's gusto and attacking inclinations when they played in the same England side, reasoning correctly that successful teams are an amalgamation of the pragmatic with flair. Boycott felt that Flintoff now gave England an extra dimension. He was a cricketer who the opposition feared because, like Botham, he could change the course of a Test match in a couple of hours.

Flintoff's bowling has a long way to go to match the variety and technical dexterity of Botham, especially before his back gave out and his pace was still extremely sharp. Comparisons between the two as bowlers are simply not valid because injuries have drastically hampered Flintoff's progress. But averaging 25 overs per Test in the West Indies is a bonus to Flintoff when you consider he never expected to be bowling at this stage of his career, given the excessive strains on his body.

When he took 5 for 58 in the Barbados Test, it was only his second 'five for' in his first-class career. After 32 Tests, he had become a genuine Test all-rounder, someone who can take five wickets in an innings and score a hundred next day. It was long overdue, but he had been an unlucky bowler for England for the past two years. The key was the addition of variety to his stock ball that

At last! I've taken five wickets in a Test for the first time. It took me 32 Tests and the wait made the moment even sweeter.

DAVID LLOYD

Former Lancashire and England coach

'Freddie captaining Lancashire? Don't do it, lad! A nest of political vipers there! But I backed him to be England captain when Nasser resigned. They always make the conservative choice and go for a batter, but you're better off with someone who also bowls and can get into the heads of his bowlers. I thought Michael Vaughan should be left alone to concentrate on his batting. Freddie has a very good cricket brain and he would have been adventurous. He's got every chance of getting the job in a few more years.'

Our lap of honour after winning in Barbados to go three-nil up. That champagne will go off with a pop once it's uncorked!

My brother, Chris (on the left) has decided that he's going to have my bottle of champagne after winning in Barbados. Our mate, Paul Beck is wondering when he can have a slurp.

We've gone three-nil up in the Test series in Barbados and it's an ecstatic England dressing-room.

is short of a length, banged in from a great height. Too often he had been used defensively, shoring up one end, giving the captain some control as runs leaked at the other end. His figures hadn't done justice to the merit of his bowling.

Just before the Barbados Test, Flintoff had a frustrating bowling stint in the nets. He was bedevilled by a no-ball problem, couldn't generate any swing and lacked rhythm. His role in the bowling line-up was clearly defined, but he felt he ought to be taking more wickets, rather than opting to bore the occasional batsman out. Flintoff sat down with the bowling coach Troy Cooley to see how he could dismiss more good players, rather than just contain. Cooley, who had quickly gained the respect of the bowlers in his first year with England, gave it to him straight. Forget about containment, pitch the ball up another yard and get at the batsmen. Attack them; impose yourself on them and forget about leaking runs. It worked straight away in Barbados.

He had Lara caught in the gully, pushing forward tentatively to a ball that was pitched up. Shivnarine Chanderpaul went to a similar delivery, caught at slip, while Ridley Jacobs and Tino Best were undone by lifters that rose alarmingly as Flintoff used his great strength to intimidate them. When he had Fidel Edwards caught behind for his fifth wicket, his roar of triumph could be heard above the din of the raucous England supporters.

'I punched the air like a footballer scoring a vital goal. It was fantastic to get that in Barbados, in front of a full house, to help bowl them out cheaply on the first day. I kept getting reminded in the press conference how long it been before I'd taken a five-for in Tests, but it wasn't for the want of trying. I now take my bowling very seriously, working hard at it but I'm still relatively inexperienced at it. Until I was about 23, I was just a bits-and-pieces bowler, but now I believe I'm a proper one, improving all the time.'

Significantly, Flintoff was usually preferred to Simon Jones as first change in the Caribbean. In fact, Jones didn't get on at all in the second innings in Barbados as Steve Harmison, Matthew Hoggard and Flintoff swept the West Indies aside for just 94. Not only did Flintoff bowl with his usual reliability, but he showed encouraging hostility. So should we now expect more wickets on a regular basis from him?

David Lloyd, his old coach, watched him closely out in the West Indies and notices he still has one glaring technical fault. 'He must work on his grip on the ball. It's set too far back in the palm of his hand. To be effective, it has to be in the tips of his fingers and thumb. If he can just release the ball at the right instant, then he'll swing it more. At the moment, he grips it like a grenade.'

Flintoff's bowling mustn't be minimised, because it kept him in the Test side for a time, until he found some batting consistency in 2002. Mike Watkinson, his coach at Lancashire believes it's no coincidence that when Flintoff is batting well, his bowling is also up to par. 'Freddie's bowling gives him subconscious support for his batting. Even if he batted at number nine for England, he'd still be a contender for a place, purely on bowling. Once he started to bowl with aggression, that has given him confidence in the other parts of his game. At the moment, his bowling is a vital component to the balance of the England attack. On a flat wicket, he can rough up the batters, and he's also not going to concede too many runs. He's been unlucky not to have a crackerjack seamer to work alongside on a regular basis who could open the wound a bit, and enable Freddie to take wickets at the other end. Perhaps that'll be Steve Harmison.

'Freddie needs to work on the off-stump area as a bowler. He can slant it in to batsmen around the thigh pad, but he doesn't get enough outside edges

Playing within myself during my hundred in the Antigua Test. The situation demanded some patience and I was delighted to prove I could play that sort of innings.

against the right-handers. That's partly due to the nature of his action and also because he worries about going for too many runs by over-attacking. But he has the capacity to swing the ball away at speed, like Courtney Walsh used to do. He needs to work more at the skill of getting the ball to hold its line when the batsman's looking for a different angle. Tactically, he's very smart as a bowler, very quick to spot a batsman's weakness and how to exploit it. He's also very comfortable at bowling around the wicket to left-handers, which bothers some fast bowlers.'

But the danger is that Flintoff could be over-bowled, so that his value as an all-rounder is diluted. When you're the Test side's main all-rounder, you can expect to bowl up to 30 overs in an innings, then be strapping on your pads within an hour if there's an early clatter of wickets. The combination of physical and mental fatigue then kicks in. How will England continue to handle Flintoff, a bowler always happy to go to the wall, sometimes to his own detriment?

Michael Vaughan, his captain, acknowledges it could be a dilemma, especially if Flintoff continues to widen his technical range and master late swing, which is always a threat to top batsmen. Flintoff's business manager, Neil Fairbrother, also wears his cricket hat when voicing his concern. 'It's a hard-working action he's got, not a smooth one like Harmison's. Freddie runs hard to the crease and delivers a muscular ball. The fact that he wants to keep running in and bowling at around 90 miles an hour is an asset to any captain, but the fact that he keeps doing it may tell against him in time. Someone else may have to do the donkey work. The plan in the 2003 South Africa series was to reduce his workload, but he ended up bowling so many overs. He needs to be looked after by England.'

Fairbrother would prefer his client eventually to be a number-five batsman for England, bowling a fair amount of overs, rather than the current punishing workload. He acknowledges the batting still has some rough edges, but his ability to dominate sets him aside from many others. 'That's an absolute must these days, for a middle-order batsman, as the Aussies demonstrate. A number five batsman has to be able to play two different ways, but he showed in Barbados that he can play within himself. His technique is sound and he can play off front and back foot, which is essential in Test cricket. He does need to work on his back-foot defence, get under the bouncer more often and move his feet a bit quicker. But it's all there. Mike Watkinson's work with him has been tremendously beneficial and in the England set-up they'll tell you how hard he works now on his batting.'

Mike Atherton thinks that number six is the ideal position for Flintoff. 'I don't think his technique will change a great deal now. He'll remain a punishing, straight-hitting batsman who'll come off now and then, giving great entertainment. He'll learn more and more about match situations, where he has to settle down a bit, but there'll be inconsistencies. He'll need to stay as the third seamer, likely to bowl around 17 overs a day, and quickly when necessary. Freddie's very important to the balance of the side, but everyone needs to realise that there'll be times when he gets himself out. I'd always have a man out at deep square leg for his instinctive hook shot. It can easily be a top edge or fly out of the ground. But good luck to him if he keeps going for it.'

John Crawley agrees with Atherton. 'His current role is perfect for the side,

MARK BUTCHER
England team-mate

'He's not just a big bloke with a big

smile on his face. There's a lot

more to him than that, he doesn't

just hit the ball as far as he can or

bowl as quickly as possible.

He's grown up a lot as a cricketer in

the past year and he thinks a lot

about what he's doing now.'

because his bowling takes pressure off his batting, and vice-versa. He also fills two places in the team. But there'll come a time when he can't bowl so many overs. Will he then slip out of the side or, like South Africa's Jacques Kallis, increase his batting skills to justify his place? That'll be a crucial career moment for Freddie. He has the potential to go a long way as a batsman. He's behind Ian Botham in terms of skill and nous as a bowler, but he can be even more destructive with the bat. He's definitely on the same level as an entertainer.'

The key to Flintoff remaining a top all-rounder is fitness. The desire is there, and he's interested in tapping into Troy Cooley's expertise to develop more bowling finesse.

'I've been quite a slow learner, much to the frustration of others as well as myself. But when I came back into the Test side for the South African series in 2003, I tried to draw a line under everything that had gone on before and start afresh. After that, I believe I improved quickly in a short space of time. I was a different player with greater self-belief and a better awareness of what I could do. I never expected my back to hold up as long as it has done, so all this is a bonus. In an ideal world, I suppose I'd do less bowling and bat higher

NEIL FAIRBROTHER
Business manager and former team-mate

'Fifteen years down the line, I fully expect

to hear people wondering who's going to

be the next Andrew Flintoff. I was still

impetuous as a batsman until I was

about 28 or 29, so he has time on his

side to settle into his game. If he's

operating at around 80 per cent at 26,

he'll be handing out a lot of punishment

when he's a little older.'

up the order, but I've got to prove myself first as a consistent batsman. All that is in the future.'

With typical clarity, Dave Roberts, the physiotherapist, explains what Flintoff has to do if he wants to remain an all-rounder, rather than someone who bats and then helps out in the bowling department. 'Unless he maintains his fitness to its present high level, he'll always be susceptible to the symptoms of that groin injury he picked up in 2002. Freddie needs to be 100 per cent fit to bowl up to 20

ABOVE Stretching for the run that brought my hundred up in the Antigua Test.

RIGHT I've got there and,my dad Colin, fiancée Rachael and my mum Susan are as pleased and relieved as me.

I'm undefeated on 102 as the England innings ends in Antigua. I'd batted almost six and a half hours, not bad for someone who was known as a fat slogger.

Enjoying our triumphs in the West Indies with my great mate, Steve Harmison. He bowled magnificently and if he keeps fit, he'll get at least 200 Test wickets. It seems a long time since we toured Pakistan together as youngsters with the Under-19s.

Trying to convince Brian Lara he's been lucky as he played me off the centre of the bat during his amazing innings in the Antigua Test. Lara wasn't fooled!

Brian Lara's 400 not out in the Antigua Test was just awesome and our congratulations were sincere. I've never seen anything like that and I'll remember it long after the pain of bowling 35 overs on a flat wicket has receded. To maintain those concentration levels for so long was incredible. Everything we tried he had an answer for. I'm glad he saved it for the final Test after we were three up.

overs a day, at the very peak of his fitness to ensure that injury never returns. He knows that; I've drilled it into him. It's like going to the dentist – if you don't brush your teeth, you'll need fillings. Freddie can have a long career as an all-rounder if he keeps himself as physically fit as he can. Otherwise he'll have to rely on his batting. That's up to Freddie. Part of his charm is that he's a loveable scamp who finds it hard to say "No" at times. He enjoys a drink and a laugh and will never be an angel. That's why the public take to him, just as they did to Beefy Botham. But he'd be daft at such a young age not to look after himself'.

This is now the best time of Flintoff's career so far. We can expect his statistics to improve after too long a period when his value to the side was not reflected in the figures. Only Tony Greig and Ian Botham can rival him as a slip fielder for England in the last 30 years. In the outfield he is deceptively fast for such a big man, with a magnificent throw. His bowling, once he grooves himself into operating off a fuller length, ought to yield him a greater crop of wickets, especially if he masters the difficult art of swinging the ball late away from the right-hander. His batting is no longer one-dimensional, as he proved in Barbados. All he needs is improved shot selection and a greater awareness of the value of keeping the scoreboard ticking over with the occasional bread-and-butter shot. Early in his innings, he is vulnerable outside the off-stump, along with many

other fine players. As Neil Fairbrother says, improved footwork ought to go some way to solving that one. He is, after all, only 26. His natural gifts are given to few, especially English, cricketers, and he must be nurtured and appreciated by those who might be tempted to confine his expansive gifts.

Flintoff has ambitions and isn't bashful to admit them. He would like to captain England at some stage. When you see how he has blossomed into a natural talisman for the younger England players in the past year, that is not too fanciful a notion. He is unselfish in the dressing-room, excellent with those who lack his naturally outgoing personality and thoughtful with those down on their luck. The change in England captaincy has brought out that constructive side in Flintoff's nature. He relates warmly to Michael Vaughan's more relaxed style of leadership.

'When Nasser was captain, you didn't want to be rooming under him. All you'd hear is the bat hitting the floor – boom! boom! boom! – and he'd prowl the hotel corridors, unable to sleep. He gave his heart and soul to the job, but

It's the day after the Antigua Test has ended and time for a spot of relaxation on the beach with some of the England supporters. After twirling a few, I'm persuaded to have a bat and proceed to get out off the first two deliveries I faced. Nothing to do with the rum punches! Graham Thorpe breathes down my neck as I safely negotiate the hat-trick ball. I would never have lived it down.

Having a go on the jetski in Antigua and
blundering around on the tennis court, giving a
few cheap laughs to some of the England boys.

that wouldn't be my way. I can switch off from cricket easily enough, but I give it my all when there's work to be done. Vaughan's the same way.'

He is full of ideas about cricket, speaks well in team meetings and isn't afraid to tell a colleague the harsh truth to his face. But he must hope that Vaughan continues growing into the job, so that the tap on the shoulder isn't likely to come until Flintoff is nudging 30 and completely at ease with his game. But he has already captained England in warm-up matches in Sri Lanka, so the management must see his leadership potential. That would have been unthinkable less than two years ago, when Flintoff was still seen as a highly talented yet brittle player, still on trial. His rehabilitation has been rapid.

Before he retires, Flintoff would love to captain Lancashire for at least a season. He accepts that England duties preclude anything other than occasional duty, but when that is done, he would like to spend at least a summer in county cricket.

'I've captained Lancashire quite a few times and really enjoyed it. But to be the full-time skipper would be a great honour. I'd love to give something back to a county I've been with since I was nine years of age. They've been very good to me.'

He has rationalised, at last, the public side of his life.

'Cricket's a game that allows you to be something that you're not. All those people shouting and clapping and you're at the centre of it all. You've got to

Resistance training in the West Indies, pulling at a bungee rope – then fooling around on the basketball court.

want it and appreciate it. Yet I'm shy, even though I'm an extrovert on the field. But I just want a quiet life away from the cricket. I get embarrassed if my family or friends talk about when I've done well, I don't like to feel I'm on parade. I want to make enough money through playing cricket and nothing else. I couldn't do all that *I'm a Celebrity* stuff in the jungle, like Phil Tufnell, or any *Hello!* magazine photo-shoots. I simply want to prove myself as a cricketer, pure and simple. Ten more years in professional cricket would be fine because every day I bowl is a bonus after what I went through.'

Although extravagantly gifted, Flintoff's progress to international prestige has

ALEX TUDOR
England team-mate

'Freddie's taken a lot of unfair stick and nonsense down the years.

He'd be the first to admit he didn't always help himself early on,

but the effort he's put in over the past three years has been unbelievable.

It's hard to take when you're just a young kid and you're told you might

never bowl again. You need a lot of character to battle through that

and look at him now. The journalists and punters haven't looked as

closely at Freddie's strength of character as they should.'

been far from serene. That's why he appreciates so much what life has given him both as a cricketer and a person. He is a genuinely charismatic presence in an England squad that is diligent and committed but with a tendency to cloned characters. Flintoff dances to a more individualistic tune while remaining a conscientious team-man. He should be allowed to grow into his vital role as England's heartbeat without anyone carping over his inevitable aberrations. Remember that next time he top-edges a hook to long leg. Do you really want to see him ducking under the bouncer for the rest of his days? There aren't enough Andrew Flintoffs in the modern game, sadly, so let's try not to clip his wings too drastically. He's bright enough to learn for himself and it should be fun watching his continuing education.

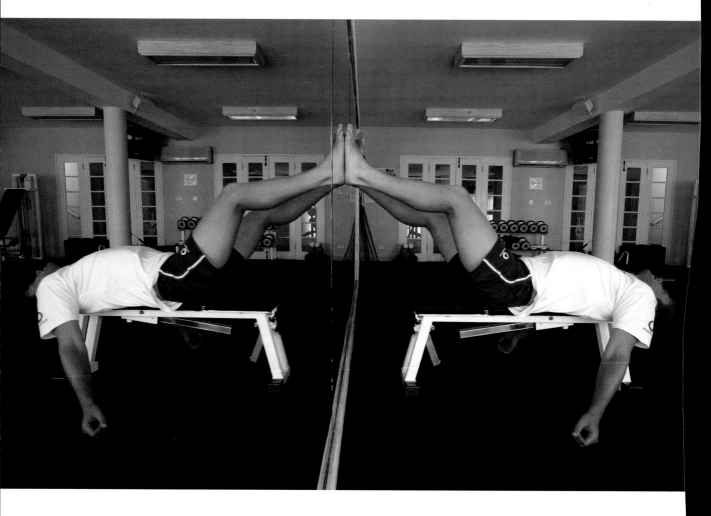

ACKNOWLEDGEMENTS

There are many I'd like to thank for getting me where I am now.
My family and my fiancée Rachael for their support and encouragement.
Also my business managers Neil Fairbrother and Chubby Chandler and
all their staff at ISM. To all those who played with me at Lancashire CCC
and everyone else at Old Trafford. The same for everyone at St Anne's CC.
Not forgetting all my England team-mates and management, as well as
four coaches who have helped me become a professional cricketer –
Jim Kenyon, John Stanworth, David Lloyd and Mike Watkinson.

My thanks also to three people who helped me produce this book –
Graham Morris for his excellent photographs, Pat Murphy for keeping
 me up far too late quizzing me about my career while working his way
through my stocks of red wine, and Myles Hodgson for helping out with
some of the interviews.

Finally, all my friends from inside and outside of the game, who have
been there for me when necessary. Too numerous to mention, but they
know who they are.

ANDREW FLINTOFF *MAY 2004*

First published in Great Britain in 2004 by Orion
a division of The Orion Publishing Group Ltd,
Orion House, 5 Upper St Martin's Lane, London
WC2H 9EA

Copyright in text © Andrew Flintoff 2004
Copyright in photographs © Graham Morris 2004

A CIP catalogue record for this book
is available from the British Library
ISBN 0-752-866567

Designed by Harry Green

Printed in Italy by Printer Trento srl